D1171923

Studies in National Policy

PERCY E. CORBETT, KENT T. HEALY,
HAROLD D. LASSWELL, JOHN P. MILLER,
EUGENE V. ROSTOW,

Editorial Committee

This series is designed to present the result of studies made in the course of an interdepartmental program of research in national policy, organized at Yale University in 1946, by members of the Departments of Economics and Political Science, and the School of Law.

A National Policy

FOR THE

Oil Industry

BY

Eugene V. Rostow

NEW HAVEN

Yale University Press

LONDON · GEOFFREY CUMBERLEGE · OXFORD UNIVERSITY PRESS

1948

For E. G. R.

ACKNOWLEDGMENTS

I am greatly indebted to my colleagues in the Yale University Seminar on National Policy, at which the substance of this monograph was presented, and to students both in the Law School and in the Graduate School, who helped immeasurably in the formulation and development of its ideas. I should like particularly to thank Kent Healy, John P. Miller, and John Spitzer, who were exceptionally patient and long-suffering critics, and Alfred Oxenfeldt, of Hofstra College, who generously contributed a detailed and incisive reading of the manuscript. In addition, Mr. Spitzer heroically volunteered for the arduous job of checking references, and Mrs. Mary E. Mansfield prepared the indices with great skill.

Funds for the publication of this volume were provided by the Carnegie Corporation, which is supporting the Yale program of research in national policy, and by the Ganson Goodyear Depew Memorial Fund of Yale University. I wish to express my gratitude to the donors and fiduciaries of these trusts.

Acknowledgment is made also to the Editors of the University of Chicago Law Review, in which passages of this manuscript appeared as parts of an article called "The New Sherman Act: Positive Instrument of Progress," in the June 1947 issue.

E. V. R.

New Haven, Connecticut,
Peru, Vermont
April 1, 1947.

Note to Third Printing

This printing corrects the text in a few details, but does not undertake to bring the material thoroughly up to date.

E. V. R.

New Haven, Connecticut
May 10, 1948.

SHORT FORM REFERENCES

The following short form citations will be used in the notes:

O'MAHONEY HEARINGS: United States Senate, Special Committee Investigating Petroleum Resources, Pursuant to S. Res. 36, 79th Cong., 1st and 2d Sess., Hearings and Reports (1945–46);

TNEC HEARINGS AND MONOGRAPHS: United States Congress, Temporary National Economic Committee, Pursuant to Pub. Res. No. 113 (75th Cong.), 76th Cong., 2d and 3d Sess., Investigation of Concentration of Economic Power (1939–41);

COOK: COOK, CONTROL OF THE PETROLEUM INDUSTRY BY THE MAJOR OIL COMPANIES, TNEC MONOGRAPH No. 39 (1941);

COLE COMMITTEE HEARINGS: United States House of Representatives, Sub-committee of the Committee on Interstate and Foreign Commerce, on H. Res. 290 and H. R. 7372, 76th Cong., 2d Sess., *Petroleum Investigation* (1939);

BAIN: J. S. BAIN, THE ECONOMICS OF THE PACIFIC COAST PETROLEUM INDUSTRY; PART I, MARKET STRUCTURE (1944);

BAIN: *id.*, PART II, PRICE BEHAVIOR AND COMPETITION (1945); Part III of Professor Bain's study, PUBLIC POLICY TOWARD COMPETITION AND PRICING (1947) became available after this paper went to press.

WATKINS: M. W. WATKINS, OIL: STABILIZATION OR CONSERVATION? (1937);

COMPACT COMMISSION: Publications of the Interstate Oil Compact Commission, State Capitol Building, Oklahoma City, Okla.

CONTENTS

PART I

OF HISTORY, GEOGRAPHY, TECHNOLOGY AND LAW

PART II

THE CONTROLS OF CRUDE OIL PRODUCTION

PART III

CONTROLLING THE PRODUCT MARKETS

PART IV

OIL ABROAD

PART V

RESTORING COMPETITION

PREFACE

THE purpose of this study is to investigate the forces which determine the level of prices and output in the petroleum industry; to examine the functioning of the system of law which defines public policy towards that industry; and to consider alternative courses of action for the industry which might be pursued in the national interest. Oil is more than one of the largest of American industries, in terms of the money, steel and men engaged in producing and selling it. Oil is an essential weapon of modern war, and oil policy must be judged ultimately from the point of view of national security.

The concern of the inquiry, moreover, is not only to analyze the petroleum industry for its own sake, but to weigh in this important instance the practical applicability of more general hypotheses about desirable national policy for the organization of industry.

The basic hypothesis of the investigation is that the organization of industry is a matter of central consequence to national policy in at least three particulars.[1] First, industrial structure is important in relation to the simple issues of economic welfare. Do petroleum products cost more than they might? Is an appropriate share of the national resources being devoted to the production of petroleum products? Is an appropriate share of the national income going to the sellers of such products? Would we get more for our money by importing more petroleum products, or exporting less?[2] Secondly, industrial organization is to be appraised in connec-

1. This paper is part of a larger inquiry into the functioning of our system of public law for the control and direction of the national economy. In the course of that study it is hoped that the hypotheses of these paragraphs will be appraised systematically and in detail.

2. The general literature about the price and output problems of large-scale industry has become formidable. It is marshalled in:

CHAMBERLIN, THEORY OF MONOPOLISTIC COMPETITION (5th ed. 1946), with supplemental bibliography (1941) 56 Q. J. ECON. 160; A. R. BURNS, THE DECLINE OF COMPETITION (1936).

tion with the trade cycle. The effect of competitive and monopolistic factors on industrial fluctuations is a matter of some controversy among economists.[3] But all parties to the debate agree that the organization of industry is one of the central problems of trade cycle theory and policy. Consideration must therefore be given to the question whether changes in the business structure could make it easier to control the trade cycle, and to maintain the economy at a high and stable level of useful employment. In the third place, and perhaps most important of all, industrial organization has sociological and political results.[4] One of the major problems requiring a social decision in our time is whether we could achieve a wider dispersal of power and opportunity, and a broader base for the class structure of our society, by a more competitive organization of this and other industries, in smaller and more independent units.

The degree of competition in the organization of industry will have a good deal to do with determining whether we

3. O. LANGE, PRICE FLEXIBILITY AND EMPLOYMENT (1944); A. P. LERNER, THE ECONOMICS OF CONTROL (1944); A. NEAL, INDUSTRIAL CONCENTRATION AND PRICE INFLEXIBILITY (1942); Bissell, *Prices, Costs and Investment* (1941) 31 AM. EC. REV. SUPP. 200; Boulding, *In Defense of Monopoly* (1945) 59 Q. J. ECON. 524, and Comments (1946) 60 Q. J. ECON. 612, 615, 619; Edwards, *The Relation of Price Policy to Fluctuations of Investment* (1938) 28 AM. EC. REV. SUPP. 56; Hansen, *Price Flexibility and Full Employment of Resources*, in National Resources Committee, The Structure of the American Economy, Part II (1940) 27; Lavington, *Monopoly and Business Stability* (1926) 6 ECONOMICA 135; Mason, *Price Policies and Full Employment*, in 1 PUBLIC POLICY (1940), ed. by C. J. FRIEDRICH and E. S. MASON, at 25; *id., Price Inflexibility* (1938) 20 REV. ECON. STAT. 53; Simons, *Economic Stability and Antitrust Policy* (1944) 11 U. OF CHI. L. REV. 338; Wallace, *Monopoly Prices and Depression*, in EXPLORATIONS IN ECONOMICS, NOTES AND ESSAYS IN HONOR OF F. W. TAUSSIG (1936), at 346. For another view, see De Haas, *Economic Peace Through Private Agreements* (1943) 22 HARV. BUS. REV. 139; J. SCHUMPETER, CAPITALISM, SOCIALISM AND DEMOCRACY (1942) ch. 8.

4. A fourth important aspect of the problem is the connection between the organization of business and the rewards of labor: the extent, that is, to which monopolistic factors in the structure of industry lead to labor "exploitation" in the economic sense. J. ROBINSON, THE ECONOMICS OF IMPERFECT COMPETITION (1933) Book 8. While it is undoubtedly true as a general proposition that elements of monopoly in the structure of the market for a commodity tend to permit the sellers of the commodity a favorable division of total income, as compared with labor less monopolistically organized, problems of wage policy have not been of special or peculiar importance in the petroleum industry, and will not be considered at length here.

remain a community long capable of social and political democracy. It should be easier to achieve the values of democracy in a society where economic power and social prestige are more widely distributed, and less concentrated, than in the United States today. Moreover, monopolistic concentration would make direct state controls, and the ultimate socialization of industry, far more likely than a regime of competitive smaller business. Concentration works towards enlarging the necessary direct economic control functions of government, and narrowing the permissible scope of private enterprise. In our society monopoly is bound in the end to be regulated or reorganized; government can safely allow it far less freedom than competitive business. Men like Mises and Hayek, and their followers, who fear and distrust the modern growth of the state and its powers, should especially favor measures to increase the importance of competitive influences in the organization of industry.[5]

One of the principal topics to be investigated, therefore, is whether in the petroleum industry, as a case in point, there are significant monopoly factors affecting market structure, and whether it would be legally and technically feasible to seek a more competitive pattern of organization for the industry.

The conclusion of this study is that the oil industry is monopolistic in its organization to an important extent; that a more competitive form of organization would be economically and socially desirable, and should be available as a practical matter under the construction of the Sherman Act which has recently been developed by the courts; and that a reorganization of the industry in the interest of competition would not involve giving up the economies of the large scale of production, or other technological advantages, but should on the contrary result in the elimination of important wastes associated with excessive size and monopoly.

In the oil industry, as in many others, the large size of the corporate units of ownership and management is not a necessity, based on technological imperatives; nor on balance does

5. See F. HAYEK, THE ROAD TO SERFDOM (1944) 35–38.

the large size of the business unit result in important technological advantages.[6] The unit of optimum efficiency in all phases of the oil industry is far smaller than the principal units of corporate organization. The bigness of the big integrated oil companies is a device to permit them to obtain the profits and security of monopoly; it has substantially nothing to do with their efficiency or their costs. A program designed to increase the competitive character of the industry would not in any sense be a turning back to an earlier era of "horse-and-buggy" technology or business. On the contrary, it would be an indispensable part of the economic policy which in our

6. The history of many corporations is the best possible evidence of the motivation for their growth. In instance after instance the motive for growth appears to have been the quest for monopoly power, not the technological advantages of scale. The formation of the Sugar Trust in the eighties, for example, involved the amalgamation of 17 refining companies, owning 20 out of 26 American refineries, representing 78 per cent of refining capacity. The companies subject to the amalgamation were capitalized at $6 million at the time of their union; the combination was capitalized at $50 million. One result of the combination was the destruction of refineries, as well as price increases. PEARCE and others, TRADE ASSOCIATION SURVEY, TNEC MONOGRAPH No. 18 (1941) 106 *ff.*; People v. North River Sugar Co., 121 N. Y. 582, 24 N. E. 834 (1890); United States v. E. C. Knight Co., 156 U. S. 1 (1895).

Similarly, in the steel industry, the component parts of the United States Steel Corporation were purchased at inflated prices, in anticipation of the profits of combination, "upon a scale that was huge and in a manner that was wild." United States v. United States Steel Corp., 223 Fed. 55, 167 (D. N. J., 1915), *aff'd.* 251 U. S. 417 (1920). Judge Woolley's conclusions—and his analysis was specifically approved by the Supreme Court, 251 U. S. at 442—was that "combinations were created by acquiring competing producing concerns at figures not based upon their physical or their business values, as independent and separate producers, but upon their values in combination; that is, upon their values as manufacturing plants and business concerns with competition eliminated. In many instances, capital stock was issued for amounts vastly in excess of the values of the properties purchased, thereby capitalizing the anticipated fruits of combination. The control acquired over the branches of the industry to which the combinations particularly related measured by the amount of production, extended in some instances from 80 per cent to 95 per cent of the entire output of the country, resulting in the immediate increase of prices, in some cases double and in others treble what they were before, yielding large dividends upon greatly inflated capital." 223 Fed. at 167.

Comparable experience can be advanced in many other industries. See, e.g., The New England Investigation, 27 I.C.C. 560 (1913), 578 *ff.*, for account of the building up of the New Haven Railroad system, involving an increase of its capitalization from $93 million to $417 million during 9 years, by financial methods which the I.C.C. characterized as "wasteful in the extreme" (p. 592); United States Bureau of Corporations, The International Harvester Co. (1913) 1–18, chs. 2–4.

present state of knowledge offers society its best chance of meeting the universal demand for full employment and economic security, without ceasing to be free.[7] For it is my own view, though the issue will not be fully canvassed here, that a more competitive organization of business should help to make the swings of the trade cycle less severe, to enlarge the number of private investment opportunities and greatly to facilitate the task of trade cycle control. A competitive economy should be more responsive than a monopolistic one to government programs designed to maintain and expand the level of national income. A greater degree of competition in industrial organization should reduce the burden of economic enterprise falling on a modern government.

Our laws controlling the petroleum industry are a fantastic and inordinately complicated patchwork of State and federal regulation, and of industrial self-regulation.[8] They rest on a premise of constitutional law which is no longer tenable: namely, the proposition that mining is not "commerce among the several States," and therefore that the production of oil is outside the power of the federal government. Our system of oil law is wasteful and expensive; its consequences have no connection with its avowed purposes. It permits and strengthens monopolistic patterns of policy for an industry which, in an appropriate legal environment, might serve the community as a model of the social and economic benefits of competition.

In view of the richness and quality of the literature about oil, this book has a restricted purpose. Except as made desirable by the accumulation of recent data, it attempts to

7. For aspects of the conception of policy out of which an economic program for American democracy can be built see M. POLANYI, FULL EMPLOYMENT AND FREE TRADE (1945); W. H. BEVERIDGE, FULL EMPLOYMENT IN A FREE SOCIETY (1944), [and review by Simons (1945) 53 J. POL. ECON. 212]; G. CROWTHER, ECONOMICS FOR DEMOCRATS (1939); S. FINE, PUBLIC SPENDING AND POST WAR ECONOMIC POLICY (1944); B. WOOTTON, FREEDOM UNDER PLANNING (1945).

8. A useful bibliography of materials on the oil industry appears in COOK, 53–55.

avoid going over ground well described in earlier work by Ise, Stocking and Watkins. It is planned rather as an essay, to evaluate the possibilities of a positive oil policy in the public interest, giving to the criteria of public interest a specific definition, and specific content, in the light of the law, economics, technology and politics of the problem.

PART I

OF HISTORY, GEOGRAPHY,
TECHNOLOGY AND LAW

THE strategic factors in the control of the oil industry, like other branches of strategy, are determined by geography, technology and history. The organization of the industry, and the curious system of habits, customs and legal rules which have developed to give it shape, are unintelligible except in terms of its particular institutional history, and of its particularized problems of market control.

CHAPTER 1

Majors and Independents

THE familiar history of the petroleum industry is of considerable importance to its present structure, and to the dynamics of its private and public procedures for making policy.

The production of oil and the refining of some oil products —mainly kerosene for lighting, and lubricants—began in 1859 in Pennsylvania. It received its first great stimulus, like so much of our industrial revolution, from the economic pressure of war—in this case, the Civil War.

By 1870 or thereabouts, the personality of John D. Rockefeller began to exert a material impact on American life. At that time Rockefeller was in the oil refining business on a moderate scale. He merged three partnerships into an Ohio corporation known as the Standard Oil Company of Ohio. The new corporation refined about 10 per cent of capacity, and had about 250 competitors, but it was the largest refining unit in the industry. During the next decade, by methods of growth which were regarded as "abnormal" even in those buccaneering days, the Standard Oil Company came to control the pipe lines which led from the Pennsylvania oil fields to the refineries in Ohio, Pennsylvania and New York. It ended up with 90 per cent of the business of producing, shipping, refining and selling petroleum products. The companies and separate business groups which had been absorbed into the Standard Oil Company combination were controlled during the eighties by a group of trustees, who held stock or other effective managerial power for forty or more component corporations, various firms and other property used in the common venture.[9]

9. Standard Oil Co. of New Jersey v. United States, 221 U. S. 1 (1911); United States Bureau of Corporations, Report of the Commissioner of Corporations on the Petroleum Industry (1907) 2 vols.; *id.*, Report of the Commissioner of Cor-

The Standard Oil Trust was of course a prototype for the popular resentment which led to the passage of the Sherman Act. Its basic policy was to retain a good deal of the individuality of the component units, but to forbid competition between them, by dividing the market geographically, and giving each unit a regional monopoly. The imprint of this essential principle of company policy survives to this day.

In 1892 the Supreme Court of Ohio declared the trust illegal, and ordered its dissolution.[10] At that time it controlled 84 companies, and a variety of other business property. The defendants complied with the Ohio decree in form, but not in fact. The dissolution of the trust was nominal, and all its essential control functions were continued. Contempt proceedings were instituted in the Ohio courts in 1897. The response of the Rockefeller group was the classic maneuver of the times. Taking advantage of the essential weakness of our divided system for controlling business, they migrated to one of the states (in this instance New Jersey) which was seeking to attract incorporation by relaxing earlier restrictions on corporate freedom. The charter of the New Jersey Standard Oil Company was amended in 1899 to make it essentially a great holding company. The first basic federal anti-trust proceeding against the Standard Oil Company was begun in 1906. Its result, in 1911, was the celebrated opinion of Mr. Justice White, announcing the "rule of reason" for interpreting Section 1, and perhaps also Section 2 of the Sherman Act.[11]

In the perspective of intellectual history, the controversy among the judges was an important one. Taft and Peckham on one side, and White on the other, were the chief spokesmen in a debate as to whether the Sherman Act really meant what it

porations on the Transportation of Petroleum (1906); A. Nevins, John D. Rockefeller; The Heroic Age of American Enterprise (1940); I. Tarbell, The History of the Standard Oil Company (1904); J. Ise, The United States Oil Policy (1926), chs. 2–5, 18–19.

10. State *ex. rel.* Watson v. Standard Oil Company, 49 Ohio St. 137, 30 N. E. 279 (1892).

11. Standard Oil Company of New Jersey v. United States, 221 U. S. 1 (1911), and 173 Fed. 177 (C. C. Mo. 1909). For text of statute see Appendix, p. 149.

said in declaring illegal every contract, combination and conspiracy in restraint of trade, whether in the form of trust or
otherwise.[12] The *Standard Oil* case, that marmoreal period
piece of Edwardian eloquence, was the triumph of White's
view, with the result of greatly enlarging the courts' freedom
to uphold business arrangements in restraint of trade.

As so often, the winning doctrine developed in a losing
case. The emphasis in the Court's opinion was on freedom of
contract, not on freedom of competition in the market. The
Sherman Act was not conceived as a weapon for assuring
society the economic and social advantages of competition in
the organization of economic life. Rather, it was interpreted as
declaring a series of ethical rules for the protection of the individual in the competitive struggle. So long as competitors
did not use what the Supreme Court regarded as morally re-
pulsive tactics—the exclusion of competitors, rebates, stealing,
or gouging—the Sherman Act itself set no limit on the results.[13] Size, the Court remarked later, was not itself an offense
under the Sherman Act, or the law would permit every form
of competition but success.[14] If monopoly resulted from the
battle of competitors, that merely confirmed the optimistic
Darwinian principles which philosophers of the time, like
Holmes himself, saw working beneath the surface of things.
The fittest survived, and the laws of progress were duly served
by the laws of men. Actually, Mr. Justice White concluded,

12. United States v. Trans-Missouri Freight Assn., 166 U. S. 290 (1897);
United States v. Addyston Pipe & Steel Co., 85 Fed. 271 (C.C.A. 6th, 1898);
Northern Securities Co. v. United States, 193 U. S. 197 (1904); Cline v. Frink
Dairy Co., 274 U. S. 445 (1927).

13. "The prohibition was suggested by the trusts, the objection to which, as
every one knows, was not the union of former competitors, but the sinister
power exercised or supposed to be exercised by the combination in keeping
rivals out of the business and ruining those who already were in." Holmes, J.,
dissenting in Northern Securities Co. v. United States, 193 U. S. 197, 405 (1904).
The great Holmes' views on Sherman Act questions were violent. "I don't dis-
guise my belief," he wrote to Pollock, "that the Sherman Act is a humbug based
on economic ignorance and incompetence." HOLMES-POLLOCK LETTERS (1941)
vol. 1, p. 163.

14. United States v. United States Steel Corporation, 251 U. S. 417 (1920);
United States v. International Harvester Co., 274 U. S. 693 (1927).

"more accurate economic conceptions" [15] led to the conviction that if restraints of trade were forbidden, monopoly was impossible. "Freedom of the individual right to contract when not unduly or improperly exercised was the most efficient means for the prevention of monopoly, since the operation of the centrifugal and centripetal forces resulting from the right to freely contract was the means by which monopoly would be inevitably prevented if no extraneous or sovereign power imposed it and no right to make unlawful contracts having a monopolistic tendency were permitted." [16]

The place of the *Standard Oil* case in the history of Sherman Act doctrine is so important that far too little attention has been given to its possibilities in the development of remedies for enforcing the Sherman Act. This was a case in which the court decreed not an injunction against offensive trade practices, but far-reaching divestments of stock by an offending holding company. It is true that the decree was inexpertly drawn, and rests on a totally inadequate analysis of the economic problems of controlling the market for petroleum products. Nonetheless it was a start, and a promising start, in the use of the most promising of all the remedies available for accomplishing the competitive reorganization of particular industries, and notably of the petroleum industry.

The decree, and its subsequent modifications, separated the Standard Oil Company of New Jersey from 37 of its chief subsidiaries and affiliates. [17] The parent company was enjoined from voting or collecting dividends on its stock in such corporations. The net result of the decree was to divide the Standard Oil Company into a series of companies, each of which was supreme in a particular geographical area. Each such company operated in all four of the main branches of the petroleum industry—production, refining, transportation and distribution. Common ownership of the stock of the separate companies has limited, but not altogether prevented the grad-

15. Standard Oil Company of New Jersey v. United States, 221 U. S. 1, 55 (1911).
16. *Id.*, 62.
17. *Id.*, 45–46.

ual development of some competition between units of the
former Standard Oil combination. The decree imposed a partial prohibition on the amalgamation of such units. The merger
of the Socony and the Vacuum Oil Companies was approved
in 1931, under the decree, but further recombination has not
been notable.[18]

The plan of organization resulting from the decree in the
Standard Oil case has remained basic in the industry. The
strong, separate regional Standard Oil companies, all integrated, and almost entirely non-competitive, have been the
polar forces in the market. They have provided the necessary
strength and machinery for price leadership and policy leadership of all kinds in an expanding, profitable, dynamic and occasionally explosive industry.[19]

After the Standard Oil decree of 1911, new companies in
no way affiliated with the Standard Oil interests grew rapidly.
The most important of them were, like the Standard companies, vertically integrated, and operated in all four phases of
the industry. There are now perhaps 22 such major integrated
companies in the oil industry, 8 of them being former units of
the Standard Oil empire. The largest of the major companies
is the Standard Oil Company (New Jersey), with over $2 bil-
lion in assets. The other majors range in size from Cities Serv-

18. United States v. Standard Oil Company of New Jersey, 47 F. (2d) 288
(D. Mo. 1931). The relative position of the Standard Oil companies in the in-
dustry has been intensively scrutinized by the Federal Trade Commission, A
Report on Prices, Profits, and Competition in the Petroleum Industry, 1927 (S.
Doc. No. 61, 70th Cong., 1st Sess. 1928), and Report on the Price of Gasoline in
1915 (1917). See also BURNS, THE DECLINE OF COMPETITION (1936) 93–109; WAT-
KINS, 22–24; National Resources Committee, The Structure of the American
Economy, Part I (1939) 311, emphasizing the continuity of Rockefeller common
stock control.

19. Federal Trade Commission, A Report on Profits, Prices, and Competition
in the Petroleum Industry, 1927 (S. Doc. No. 61, 70th Cong., 1st Sess., 1928) chs.
4–7. During the last thirty-five years the Standard Oil companies have lost a
good deal of their relative power, and their unity of policy has been relaxed.
Other great companies, created in their image, share the burden of policy formation. Nonetheless they have been, and still are, dominating elements in the structure of business and market organization. Their existence has probably been a
major factor determining the evolution of the oil companies in a form so different, for example, than the pattern which prevails in the coal or even the steel
industries.

ice Company, with about $1 billion in assets, to the Skelly Oil Company, with total assets of about $62 million, Barnsdall Oil Company, whose total assets are $25.7 million, and Standard Oil Company (Kentucky), $42.6 million.[20] Between 5 to 16 such companies operate in any one retail marketing area, the modal number being 11. Independent companies, usually non-integrated or semi-integrated, exist in every phase of the industry except transportation.

20. COOK, 3–4; see also, TNEC MONOGRAPH NO. 39a, REVIEW AND CRITICISM ON BEHALF OF STANDARD OIL CO. (NEW JERSEY) AND SUN OIL CO. OF MONOGRAPH NO. 39, WITH REJOINDER BY MONOGRAPH AUTHOR (1941). Subsequent data are given in O'MAHONEY HEARINGS, *The Independent Petroleum Company* (1946) 51–65, 518 *ff.*; and see United States Senate, Special Committee to Study Problems of American Small Business, Report of the Smaller War Plants Corporation, *Economic Concentration and World War II*, 79th Cong., 2d Sess. (1946), 165–171. The question "what is a major oil company" admits some argument. Twenty-two companies are listed as fully integrated majors in the complaint in United States v. American Petroleum Institute, Civil Action No. 8524 (D. Col. 1940) 29–30, now pending. Apart from slight statistical variations between reports, the differences are immaterial.

CHAPTER 2

The Structure of the Market

THE geography and technology of the petroleum industry
are simple but not fixed. Oil is produced from the ground in
24 states of the Union, of which Texas, with 44.6 per cent of
1944 production, and California with 18.6 per cent, are now
the most important, followed by Louisiana, with 7.7 per cent,
Oklahoma with 7.4 per cent, Kansas with 5.9 per cent, Illinois
with 4.6 per cent, and other states lesser amounts.[21] Oil flows
from the producing areas in three main streams—from the
ports of the Gulf of Mexico by sea to the Eastern seaboard;
from the Mid-Continent area of Kansas, Oklahoma and
Northern Texas north by pipeline and rail to the great industrial and population centers of the northern Middle West;
from the California fields to West Coast and transpacific markets.

These flows of oil are not immutable, even in the sense that
movements of soft coal or iron ore are determined by geography, and help to determine the location of industry. New
oil fields can be discovered at any moment—off shore, or in
the tremendous areas of the United States which geologists
say are likely to contain oil. Improvements in the technique of
using the oil shales of Wyoming, or the tarry oils of central
Canada, or the soft coal of the Middle South, could equally
change the pattern of supply and distribution of liquid fuels.
The very rapid recent rise in the making of gasoline from nat-

21. O'MAHONEY HEARINGS, *Investigation of Petroleum Resources* (1945)
42; United States Department of the Interior, Bureau of Mines, Minerals Yearbook 1944 (1946) 1081. The table given in the Minerals Yearbook indicates some
change in the pattern of distribution of production during the war years. In
1935, California's percentage was 20.9 per cent, in 1937, 18.6 per cent, whereas
Texas produced 39.4 per cent in 1935 and 39.9 per cent in 1937. Oklahoma, on
the other hand, has dropped steadily from 18.8 per cent in 1936.

ural gas threatens a revolutionary change in the supply of liquid fuels.[22] Changes in tariffs, or in cost conditions abroad, or further price rises in the United States uncompensated in the rates of exchange, could bring Middle Eastern oil to New York as well as the small trickle of Venezuelan oil now favored by a special trade agreement concession. Alternatively, the development of oil production in the Middle East may lead to a displacement of South American oil products in Europe, and their insistent appearance on the North American market. Radical changes in the cost of transportation—for example, the utilization of the new pipelines built during the war— could shift the shares of the several producing areas in the business of great markets.

For present purposes, however, we can take it as a datum that oil comes from about 400,000 wells in the United States, the most important of which are located in three producing areas.[23] Each of the three chief areas of production has a preferential, though not by any means a monopoly position in the three chief areas of consumption. The markets are somewhat insulated from each other, although movements of crude oil are decidedly sensitive to small differentials in the cost of transportation. Occasionally the markets are linked also by factors of intercorporate warfare. Thus Standard of California has recently entered the New England area, by way of reprisal for a foray into California made by Socony-Vacuum, its sibling of the Standard family.

Twenty-one major integrated companies owned 29.4 per cent of the producing oil wells in 1944, and produced about 61.3 per cent of the crude oil. In 1939, those companies owned 27.6 per cent of the producing wells, and produced only 52.2 per cent of the crude oil.[24] However, they own over 70 per

22. O'MAHONEY HEARINGS, *Investigation of Petroleum Resources* (1945) 54–56; 26; 506–532; 320–321. Generally on alternative sources of oil, see 47–54; 317–409.

23. O'MAHONEY HEARINGS, *Petroleum Requirements—Postwar* (1945) 42.

24. O'MAHONEY HEARINGS, *The Independent Petroleum Company* (1946) 51–52. See also United States House of Representatives, Special Committee to Conduct a Study and Investigation of the National Defense Program in its Relation to Small Business in the United States, pursuant to H. Res. 18, 78th Cong.,

cent of the proven reserves of oil.[25] The major companies' ownership of reserves on so large a scale has been a recent development, stimulated by fears of shortages, and by the structure of the tax laws, which have made ownership of reserves advantageous taxwise. Despite the scale of major company ownership of reserves, it is comparatively rare for any one company to own an entire field.

The oil from the 400,000 oil wells is transported to about 600 refineries for processing. It gets there in boats, railway tank cars, pipe lines and trucks, and often by a combination of routes. The refineries, and especially the refineries of the major companies, are usually located in the consuming areas, not in the areas of production, so as to be partially protected against obsolescence in the event of a shift in source of supply from one oil field to a new one. Thus control of transportation facilities, as well as of refining facilities, is a vital factor in the control of petroleum product prices. In 1938, 15 of the major companies owned 87.2 per cent of the tankers; in 1939, 16 of them owned 96.1 per cent of the gasoline pipe lines; in 1938, 14 majors owned 89 per cent of the trunk pipe lines transporting crude oil to the refineries.[26] In 1945, 21 majors held 82 per cent of crude oil refining capacity as compared with 75.8 per cent in 1940. Nineteen of the major companies made over 83 per cent of the crude runs to stills in 1944, compared with 80.9 per cent in 1940.[27] Six of the major companies own about 45 per cent of crude-oil refining capacity, and over 53 per cent of cracking capacity.[28]

From the refineries, petroleum products go to market through a variety of channels—by direct sales to large con-

---

2d Sess., Report No. 2015, *Current Problems of Independent Crude Oil Producers* (1944).

25. COOK, 10.
26. *Id.*, 5.
27. O'MAHONEY HEARINGS, *The Independent Petroleum Company* (1946) 52.
28. COOK, 31. Current percentages are undoubtedly higher. O'MAHONEY HEARINGS, *Wartime Petroleum Policy under the Petroleum Administration for War* (1945) 136; Report of the Surplus Property Administration, Aviation-Gasoline Plants and Facilities (Jan. 14, 1946) 30-31; United States Senate, *loc. cit. supra* note 20, 169-170.

sumers, through tied or independent wholesale jobbers, or through the refining company's own retail distribution system to ultimate consumers. At the present time gasoline is the chief product of the petroleum industry, although oil for heating, bunkers, and engines, asphalt, and lubricants are all important, and chemicals, synthetics and rubber loom up as possible future products on a large scale. The major companies own 73 per cent of all bulk plants for the handling and storage of gasoline in consuming centers, and about 40 per cent of all service stations. Of 8,000 wholesale jobbers, 80 per cent have binding contracts with a single major company supplier. This has not always been true of the industry, and is an area of practice where a positive relaxation of legal restrictions has been a real factor in facilitating market control through tying arrangements.[29]

The selling of gasoline and of other petroleum products is everywhere characterized by the kind of competitive behavior which would be expected in a market of a few sellers.[30] There is a pronounced fear of "spoiling the market," and a corresponding disinclination to undertake open price competition. Each large seller knows that its share of market supply is a significant fraction of total supply. It realizes therefore that price changes on its part would be met by comparable price changes on the part of its competitors. Thus a price cut could not be expected to change any large seller's share of the market, but

29. Cook, 41–50. The figures refer to the period immediately before the war. The complaint in United States v. American Petroleum Institute (No. 8524, D. Col. 1940), alleges that the 22 major companies own or control 75 per cent of all service stations. A witness for the industry asserted that major company ownership of filling stations was about 15 per cent. TNEC Hearings, Part 15, 8415. See O'Mahoney Hearings, *The Independent Petroleum Company* (1946) 532–564; TNEC Hearings, Part 16, 9127 ff.; Part 15A; Part 17, 9737–9742; Part 15, 8396–8456.

30. This is not to suggest that small numbers is the only significant element in price policy, or that variations in the pattern of market behavior common for markets dominated by a few large buyers or sellers do not take place. Chamberlin, Theory of Monopolistic Competition (5th ed., 1946) chs. 3–6; Sweezy, *Demand under Conditions of Oligopoly* (1939) 47 J. Pol. Econ. 568; Machlup, *Marginal Analysis and Empirical Research* (1946) 36 Am. Ec. Rev. 519; Wilcox and others, Competition and Monopoly in American Industry, TNEC Monograph No. 21 (1940); Nelson and Keim, Price Behavior and Business Policy, TNEC Monograph No. 1 (1940), especially Part I, ch. 3, and Parts II and III.

could be expected to reduce everyone's level of profit. In a large seller's calculations, therefore, the only possible justification for a price cut would be to take advantage of the elasticity of demand, which under various circumstances might be enough to offset the impact on profits of a lower price.

But the large sellers of petroleum products generally believe that the demand for their products, and especially the demand for gasoline, is notably inelastic. This conviction is of course a typical article of faith among monopolistic sellers. It is an idea essential to the stability of a price system in which price competition is regarded as unethical, at best, and often vaguely criminal as well. The fact is that the market for petroleum products is decidedly sensitive to price changes. As in other market contexts, elasticity of demand is not a simple or a continuous mathematical function. Market response to upward movements of price may be generally different than its response to price cuts. Gasoline is usually bought for prompt use, storage even for industrial consumers being expensive and limited. Thus forward buying by consumers in anticipation of price changes is of limited importance to the market. At different stages of the trade cycle, the quantity taken varies with price to different degrees, although petroleum products do not experience the extreme variations in consumption during the course of trade cycles which characterize capital goods like steel. The rate of exploration and of wildcat drilling, and hence the supply, is responsive to the level of prices. There is competition between petroleum products and other sources of energy, and between motor and other forms of transportation service, markedly influenced by relative prices. Orthodox techniques of clearing the market by reducing prices are used when sellers' inventories are built up on the basis of market guesses which turn out to be wrong. While the elasticity of demand for petroleum products is in no sense a constant, applicable mechanically to all products or at all periods of a trade cycle, it is misleading to assume that price is immaterial to demand. On the contrary, a pioneering study indicates that price is one of the important dynamic factors influencing the demand for gasoline, ranking with the level of national income and the availability of roads as an element in the shifting demand for the product.[31]

Price leadership, usually based on prices quoted by the leading local survivor of the Standard Oil Trust, is the dominant feature of price policy for gasoline, bunker oil, and to a somewhat lesser extent, for heating and other fuel oils. If a substantial seller deviates from the price posted by the market leader, all other sellers follow suit, in a process which sometimes becomes a price "war." After a time, the regime of price leadership by the largest major is restored, at a higher level of prices. Efforts of each major company to change its share of the market consist of competitive expenditure on advertising, service stations and their facilities, research to justify the claim of product differentiation (without altering the standardized quality of the product), and other costs designed to create consumer preferences for one seller's product rather than another. In the extent and variety of such behavior, the oil industry presents a nearly classic case of the wastes of monopolistic competition.

Price discrimination, as well as price leadership, is deeply established practice in the petroleum industry, both among the several petroleum products, and within the gasoline market itself.

Gasoline is the principal product of the oil industry, in volume and in market value. The adjustment of the refining process to the pressure of variations in the market demand for gasoline, heating oil, Diesel and fuel oil, and other products, is a fascinating exercise in economic calculation. These commodities are generally produced together in varying proportions, in the distillation or cracking of crude oil. There are some small cost differences attributable to additional handling and processing required for some of the products. But the prevailing differences in price bear no possible relation to differ-

31. Consult C. F. Roos, Dynamic Economics (1934) ch. 3, esp. p. 30. See also O'Mahoney Hearings, *Petroleum Requirements—Postwar* (1946) 65–66; Cole Committee Hearings, 183–188.

ences in cost. They represent a pattern of price discrimination. Jointly produced commodities are sold in different markets at different prices. The elasticity of demand for the several commodities is different, depending upon the price and availability of substitutes, the weather, the state of the trade cycle, and the other limiting elements in the demand for petroleum products. Within the gasoline market itself, price discriminations are customary between the several grades of gasoline, between branded and unbranded products, and between those branded with highly advertised or with local labels. The most careful study of the subject concludes that such differences generally do not reflect differences in costs, but represent the most profitable possible adaptation of monopolistic sellers to market forces.[32]

Such, in broad outline, is the prevailing pattern of the oil business. This dynamic structure of major and independent companies is not, however, the whole story. The companies function within a specialized framework of law which in itself has an important history.

32. 2 BAIN, 159 ff., esp. p. 165. The special component of ethyl gasoline, for example, is sold to the refiner at .37 cents per gallon [COOK, 44. Cf. 2 BAIN, 206], but the blended product customarily sells at 2 cents a gallon more than regular gas.

CHAPTER 3

The System of Oil Law

THERE are two principal and closely related themes in the history of our oil law: proposals based on ideas of preventing the waste of an exhaustible natural resource; and proposals for industrial "self-government," that is, of business combination in restraint of competition. Periods of apparent oil shortage stimulated conservation policies. And both the trade association movement of the twenties, and its period of triumph in the N.R.A., accelerated a deep-seated and typical trend towards combination. As in many other industrial situations, there is in oil the steady thrust and counterthrust of what may loosely be identified as pressures of competition and of monopoly—the quest for private control over markets by existing business units and groups on the one hand, and on the other, the quest by outsiders for increased participation in a profitable sector of the economy. Deference to the ideal of conservation is matched by interest in short-run profit. The development of both themes in oil policy was strongly stimulated by the underlying peculiarities of the rules of law governing the ownership of oil as it emerges from the earth.

Oil exists in geological formations of various kinds, in underground pools or reservoirs.[33] Such reservoirs consist of liquid oil or liquifiable oil vapors mixed with gas or water or both. The underground reservoirs exist at great pressures, and contain tremendous amounts of energy. When a drill and pipe are inserted into the underground pool, introducing a

33. A. DUNSTAN and others, THE SCIENCE OF PETROLEUM (1938) vol. 1; National Resources Committee, Energy Resources and National Policy (1939) 127–143; TNEC HEARINGS, Part 14, 7390–7423; O'MAHONEY HEARINGS, *Investigation of Petroleum Resources* (1945) 78–92, 289–405; COLE COMMITTEE HEARINGS 289–407; FANNING (ed.), OUR OIL RESOURCES (1945) chs. 4–5; United States House of Representatives, Subcommittee of Committee on Interstate and Foreign Commerce, Hearings on H. Res. 441, *Petroleum Investigation*, 73d Cong. (Recess), (1934) Part 2.

point of atmospheric pressure, oil, gas and water are driven to the point of lower pressure from all parts of the underground pool, and are propelled to the surface in mixtures of various kinds, depending on the special geological character of the reservoir.

In dealing with the questions of ownership presented by this phenomenon, the courts in the United States clung to two germinal ideas. The first was that the owner of a surface plot had some sort of an ownership claim in the oil which lay beneath his land. On the other hand, oil flowed out of an underground pool without any respect for the lines of proprietorship traced on the maps and plats of the surface. If A, owning an acre over the middle of an oil-gas reservoir, inserted a well, oil would flow to his well from under the land of B, who owned three acres over one edge of the underground pool. Oil was "fugacious," the judges said; it flowed like percolating waters, it wandered about like wild animals in the state of their natural ferocity. The courts began to rule that it belonged to the man who brought it to the surface, without reference to the point at which the flow began. The legislatures might legitimately seek to assure each surface owner a share in the take of the underlying pool in some proportion to the richness of the part of the pool under his tract—that is, they might seek to protect the so-called "correlative" interests of the surface owners in the oil beneath their lands—but, so far as the courts were concerned, the starting point of the common law of oil was the rule of capture.[34]

The economic effects of the rule were unsettling, to say the least. If A put down a well, his neighbor B had to do likewise, or run the risk of losing all "his" oil to A. If A continued to produce and sell at low prices, B was in harness too, and found it hard to stop unless he was willing to face the loss of the total

34. Westmoreland and Cambria Nat. Gas Co. v. DeWitt, 130 Penn. St. 235, 18 Atl. 724 (1889); Ohio Oil Co. v. Indiana, 177 U. S. 190 (1900); Lindsley v. Natural Carbonic Gas Co., 220 U. S. 61 (1911). American Bar Association, Mineral Law Section, Legal History of Conservation of Oil and Gas (1939); Marshall and Meyers, *Legal Planning of Petroleum Production* (1931) 41 YALE L. J. 33, (1933) 42 *id.* 702; Ely, *The Conservation of Oil* (1938) 51 HARV. L. REV. 1209.

capital value of his expected future recoveries. At the same time the exploitation of oil reserves under the rule of capture was accompanied by spectacular wastes. For example, gas emerging with the oil, especially in the initial gusher flow of a pool, was burned off; or the pool was allowed to produce at maximum flow, which used up the propulsive pressure of the gas in the pool at a rapid rate. The courts early held that the states had a strong interest in protecting society against the waste of oil and gas, and could therefore require the production of oil to conform to rules of practice established in the interest of conservation: prohibitions, for instance, against burning gas as it was blown out of oil wells, or allowing it to be dissipated into the air, and the like.

During and after the last war fears of an oil shortage, and international friction over oil, led to the development of more comprehensive statutes in the interest of conservation. The first prorationing statute was passed in 1914, although the effective development and enforcement of this kind of statute was not attempted until after the discoveries of the late twenties and early thirties. Prorationing statutes purport to limit the production of each well to a fraction of its potential production, the determination of the fraction presumably taking equitable cognizance of the differing geological properties of the different tracts above the reservoir. They also declare rules of conservation practice in the extraction of oil, having to do with the use of reservoir gas pressure, the spacing of wells, and other problems.[35]

In 1924 President Coolidge established a Federal Oil Conservation Board to recommend a national policy for the oil

35. See note 34 *supra*, and Federal Oil Conservation Board, Ely (ed.), The Oil and Gas Conservation Statutes, Annotated (1933); Moses, *The Constitutional, Legislative and Judicial Growth of Oil and Gas Conservation Statutes* (1941) 13 Miss. L. J. 353; Summers, *The Modern Theory and Practical Application of Statutes for the Conservation of Oil and Gas* (1938) 13 Tulane L. Rev. 1; Davis, *Judicial Emasculation of Administrative Action and Oil Proration* (1940) 19 Tex. L. Rev. 29; Davis and Willbern, *Administrative Control of Oil Production in Texas* (1944) 22 Tex. L. Rev. 149; Hardwicke, *Oil Conservation: Statutes, Administration and Court Review* (1941) 13 Miss. L. J. 381; Comment, *Proration of Petroleum Production* (1942) 51 Yale L. J. 608; Note, *Administrative Regulation of Petroleum Production* (1946) 59 Harv. L. Rev. 1142.

industry, in view of the expected shortages of oil, and of concern over the waste of petroleum in the process of its extraction and manufacture. The Board was properly doubtful of the possibilities of federal regulation of oil production, in the face of the then state of constitutional law. Its proposals, therefore, were that the states work actively to develop conservation statutes, backed by interstate cooperation, and by the technical and advisory assistance of the federal government, chiefly through the Department of Interior.[36]

The Seminole Field in Oklahoma was discovered in 1926, and the fear of an oil shortage faded. Suddenly the industry began to talk about "over-production," and to worry actively about the possibility of limiting the production of oil to "market demand."

The twenties were the palmy days of the trade association. Actively backed by the Department of Commerce and in the case of oil by the Department of Interior as well, trade associations were promoted as the panacea of business, the new and rational model of enlightened competition, the vision of order and cooperation, as compared with the dark and primitive practices of cutthroat competition, fit only for the life of the jungle. The Federal Trade Commission, though more suspicious, sponsored a series of "trade-practice" conferences, for which high hopes of business rationality were entertained.[37] The American Petroleum Institute, the trade association of the industry, proposed plans for world-wide self-regulation of the industry, whose basic purpose was to limit production to "demand." The Federal Oil Conservation Board submitted this proposal to the Attorney-General, whose opinion was sharply critical. In the light of the Attorney-General's reaction, the Oil Conservation Board in 1929 proposed that oil

36. Federal Oil Conservation Board, Report to the President, Part I (1926) 13–25; Report IV (1930); Report V (1932) 1–4, and App. II. See also Report III (1929); N. ELY, OIL CONSERVATION THROUGH INTERSTATE AGREEMENT (1933); WATKINS, chs. 5–7.

37. Such a code for the oil industry, at least in its marketing phases, was proposed by the American Petroleum Institute and, as modified, adopted by the Federal Trade Commission. Federal Trade Commission, Trade Practice Conferences (1933) 48–51. See WATKINS, 45–46.

controls be sought through the effective cooperation of the interested states, with the aid of the Federal Government. Parallel state laws designed to limit production, and their coordination through interstate action, was the basic technique advanced by Secretary Wilbur.[38]

Meanwhile the general depression began, in 1929 and 1930, and hit the oil industry with peculiar force. For while the demand for petroleum products declined, as national income was reduced, two great new oil fields were discovered in California and in East Texas. A vast supply of cheap oil gushed out of the earth, imposing a new downward pressure on prices, and on the profitability of oil production in the older fields. At the same time the federal courts began to enjoin the enforcement of state prorationing statutes, which had developed in response to the work of the Federal Oil Conservation Board, the proposals of the industry, the cooperative activities of the governors of the chief oil producing states, and the force of circumstance.[39]

Manifestly, no prorationing plan of limiting production can be enforced by a single state unless it has a monopoly of the commodity in question.[40] The effective development of the prorationing device required interstate cooperation at the least. By 1930, at the request of the Federal Oil Conservation Board, voluntary committees of the oil industry, working with the Bureau of Mines of the Department of Interior, developed over-all estimates of the demand for petroleum, to serve as the production targets of the state prorationing systems. In 1931, the Governors Oil States Advisory Committee met to contemplate coordinated action by the producing states, in view of the rapid fall of prices, and the frustration of state regulatory efforts by the lower federal courts. This group persevered in

38. N. Ely, Oil Conservation through Interstate Agreement (1933) 17–25; Ford, *Controlling the Production of Oil* (1932) 30 Mich. L. Rev. 1170; Comment (1935) 45 Yale L. J. 324, 332.

39. MacMillan v. Railroad Commission of Texas, 51 F. (2d) 400 (W. D. Tex. 1931), *dismissed as moot* 287 U. S. 576 (1932); People's Petroleum Producers, Inc. v. Smith, 1 F. Supp. 361 (E. D. Tex. 1932).

40. For a striking illustration of state restrictive regulation, imposing monopoly prices for raisins on the national economy, see Parker v. Brown, 317 U. S. 341 (1943).

its efforts to fulfill the broad policy declared by the Federal Oil Conservation Board—state restrictions of production, backed by interstate cooperation and federal assistance. In Texas and Oklahoma, the crisis of oil control reached such a pitch of confusion that the governors declared martial law, and called out the National Guard to enforce the state prorationing statutes.[41]

In 1932, the Supreme Court declared prorationing legal,[42] and a year later held the use of troops under the circumstances to have been illegal.[43] Meanwhile, in 1933, the N.R.A. began, for oil as for other industries, a lastingly important period of strengthened monopoly influences.[44]

The Oil Code under N.R.A. was created out of the prevailing institutions and ideas of the industry. The basic device used in the Code was control of production by state prorationing. The object of the production control policy was to restore a so-called parity price for crude oil, which emerged from the high-sounding and pseudo-scientific formula of the Code at the convenient rule of thumb figure of $1 a barrel.[45]

In order to make state limitations of production effective,

41. Constantin v. Smith, 57 F. (2d) 227 (E. D. Tex. 1932); Russell Petroleum Co. v. Walker, 162 Okla. 216, 19 P. (2d) 582 (1933). Marshall and Meyers, *Legal Planning of Petroleum Production* (1931) 41 YALE L. J. 33, 52 ff.

42. Champlin Refining Co. v. Corporation Commission of Oklahoma, 286 U. S. 210 (1932).

43. Sterling v. Constantin, 287 U. S. 378 (1932). FAIRMAN, THE LAW OF MARTIAL RULE (2d ed. 1943) 99 ff.; Comment (1936) 45 YALE L. J. 879.

44. WATKINS, chs. 7–11; R. WILLIAMSON, THE POLITICS OF PLANNING IN THE OIL INDUSTRY UNDER THE CODE (1936); National Recovery Administration, National Recovery Review Board, 2d Report to the President (1934) 62–67; S. WHITNEY, TRADE ASSOCIATIONS AND INDUSTRIAL CONTROL (1934); Department of the Interior, Annual Report (1934) 11–20; *id.*, Annual Report (1935) 29–42; *id.*, Petroleum Administrative Board, Final Report, Marketing Division (1936); Meyers, *Petroleum Industry*, in M. HANDLER, CASES ON TRADE REGULATION (1937) at 1196.

45. National Recovery Administration, Code of Fair Competition for the Petroleum Industry (1933), Art. III; United States v. Socony-Vacuum Oil Co., 105 F. (2d) 809, 817 (C.C.A. 7th, 1939), *reversed* United States v. Socony-Vacuum Oil Co., 310 U. S. 150 (1940); WATKINS, 135–138. The average price for crude oil at the wells during the period 1936–39 was $1.105 per barrel. United States House of Representatives, Hearings before Select Committee on H. Res. 64, 79th Cong., 1st Sess., *A Study and Investigation of the National Defense Program in Its Relation to Small Business* (1945) Part 3, 1386–1387.

two steps were taken. First, the forecasts of demand, which had been begun some time before, were taken over as a function of the Petroleum Administrative Board, a body appointed to advise the Secretary of Interior, in his capacity as Administrator of the Oil Code, and to act for him in duties which he assigned to it. During the Code period, the Bureau of Mines itself began to make the forecasts, rather than simply to advise an industry committee on their preparation.[46] These monthly forecasts of demand for petroleum began to emerge as the key step in the process of controlling production.

The second device developed under the National Recovery program to make production controls effective was the federal prohibition against shipments in interstate commerce of oil produced in violation of state production control laws.[47] This delegation of the Congress' responsibility for the state of national commerce put a powerful sanction behind the state prorationing laws. For the first time the states were in a position effectively to control the supply of oil on the national market, and hence its price. This feature of the National Recovery Act was reenacted by Congress as emergency legislation after the Supreme Court had invalidated Section 9 (c) of the National Recovery Act, and the regulations promulgated under it, and it has now become a permanent part of the Federal Code.[48]

The Code period also powerfully stimulated the organization of procedures to assure common and concerted action on the part of the oil-producing states. The occasional meetings of the Governors of the oil-producing states gave way to a permanent Commission, established by an interstate compact

46. TNEC HEARINGS, Part 17, 9584.
47. Sec. 9 (c) of the National Recovery Act, 48 STAT. 195 (1933); Panama Refining Co. v. Ryan, 293 U. S. 388 (1935).
48. 49 STAT. 30 (1935), 15 U. S. C., § 715 (1940); President v. Skeen, 118 F. (2d) 58 (C.C.A. 5th, 1941); Griswold v. President, 82 F. (2d) 922 (C.C.A. 5th, 1936); Gibson v. Stiles, 90 F. (2d) 998 (C.C.A. 5th, 1937); 50 STAT. 257 (1937), 53 STAT. 927 (1939), 56 STAT. 381 (1942), 15 U. S. C. § 715 (1) (Supp. III, 1944); COLE COMMITTEE HEARINGS, 40–57; United States House of Representatives, Hearings before a Subcommittee of the Committee on Interstate and Foreign Commerce on S. 1302 and H. R. 4547, 2308, 76th Cong., 1st Sess., *Petroleum Shipments* (1939), particularly 84–111. The statute is popularly known as the Connally Act.

among the states, and now functioning as an agency of coordination, information and policy guidance.[49]

While this mechanism for production control was taking shape, the Anti-Trust Division of the Department of Justice was at war on the side lines in a series of important but peripheral anti-trust cases involving several phases of price policy in the oil industry.[50] Occasionally, as in the *Socony-Vacuum* case, it was in open conflict with officials of the Department of Interior. Each of its cases dealt with an aspect of the problem of market control—price practices, the control of transport facilities, the abuse of patent power, and so on. Each case was frustrated in practical results by the underlying pattern of monopolistic structure in the industry—the size and particularly the integration of the major units; their fewness in numbers in each relevant sub-market for petroleum products; and the extent to which effective monopolistic control depended upon mastery of the bottle-necks, and parallel responses based on self-interest rather than overt combination.

In 1940 a somewhat more promising case was instituted, attempting for the first time to deal with the essentials of monopolistic power in the industry as a whole.[51] That case was suspended by the war, but in 1946 was restored to the calendar,

49. 49 Stat. 939 (1935); 50 Stat. 617 (1937); 53 Stat. 1071 (1939); 55 Stat. 666 (1941); 57 Stat. 383 (1943). N. Ely, Oil Conservation through Interstate Agreement (1933); Comment (1935) 45 Yale L. J. 324, 332. The Interstate Oil Compact Commission publishes a valuable Quarterly Bulletin, and other Bulletins, in which state and federal activities in the field of oil and gas control are reported and discussed. A collection of statutes and legislative reports are found in Cole Committee Hearings, 57–64.

50. United States v. Socony-Vacuum Oil Co., 310 U. S. 150 (1940); Ethyl Gasoline Corp. v. United States, 309 U. S. 436 (1940); United States v. Atlantic Refining Co., Civil Action 14060 (D. Col. 1941), (1941) 10 U.S.L. Week 2403; Comments (1942) 51 Yale L. J. 1338, 1349 ff.; (1942) 9 U. of Chi. L. Rev. 503; United States v. Standard Oil Co. of California, In Equity No. 2542-K (N. D. Cal. 1930), Consent Decree, and modifications, set forth in United States House of Representatives, Subcommittee No. 3 of the Committee on the Judiciary, Hearings on H. R. 2318, *Oil Marketing Divorcement,* 76th Cong., 1st Sess. (1939), Serial 8, 82–86, and discussed at 74–75; United States v. General Petroleum Corp., 33 F. Supp. 95 (S. D. Cal. 1940) (plea of *nolo contendere* entered, 2 Bain 276).

51. United States v. American Petroleum Institute, Civil Action No. 8524 (D. Col. 1940), Complaint. See ch. 10 *infra.*

for negotiation and perhaps trial. At this writing (April, 1947) the proceeding has once more gone into a condition of suspense. While the scope and analysis of the industry presented in the complaint are adequate and realistic, the prayers for relief are disappointingly narrow. The complaint was drafted before the *Aluminum* and *Tobacco* cases had revolutionized the law of the Sherman Act.[52] There is grave danger that unless the complaint is amended, this case, like its recent predecessors, will fail to have an important economic effect on the main tools of monopolistic power in the oil industry.

52. United States v. Aluminum Co. of America, 148 F. (2d) 416 (C.C.A. 2d, 1945); American Tobacco Co. v. United States, 66 Sup. Ct. 1125 (U. S. 1946). See ch. 13 *infra*.

PART II

THE CONTROLS OF CRUDE
OIL PRODUCTION

THUS the corporate structure and the control structure of the oil industry have emerged, in the course of a lengthy historical experience. The company structure is dominated by the history of the Standard Oil Company and by the necessary steps in market control strategy imposed by the technology and geography of the industry. The control structure is an uneasy balance of anti-trust ideas and their antithesis, a plan for limiting supply, which works through a constitutionally remarkable blend of state and federal action. This plan has been taking shape for twenty years, and is now in fully effective operation. It deserves detailed examination.

CHAPTER 4

The Determination of Supply: Conservation and Price Factors

THE amount of crude oil produced each month is fixed by the monthly estimates of market demand published by the Bureau of Mines of the Department of Interior. These estimates are a carefully compiled statistical projection of market trends. The Bureau of Mines estimates are a crucial step in the process of controlling supply, for no state could limit its production unless it knew that its competitor states were doing likewise. The Bureau of Mines estimates work a good deal like the trade association statistical services condemned in the *Sugar Institute* and like cases under the anti-trust laws.[53] They operate to control prices by controlling supply. Spokesmen for the Bureau of Mines are vehement in denying that their forecasts have anything to do with price control.[54] Yet there is no such thing in business life as demand apart from price, and daily experience in the industry confirms the view that the demand for oil products is a function of price as well as other factors.[55] The Bureau of Mines forecasts of demand depend on the concealed premise of price stability. Their effect is to state how much or how little crude oil need be produced to permit prices to remain fixed.

53. American Column & Lumber Co. v. United States, 257 U. S. 377 (1921); Maple Flooring Manufacturers Ass'n. v. United States, 268 U. S. 563 (1925); Sugar Institute, Inc. v. United States, 297 U. S. 553 (1936); Hartford-Empire Co. v. United States, 323 U. S. 386, 427 (1945). Fly, *Observations on the Anti-Trust Laws, Economic Theory and the Sugar Institute Decisions: I* (1936) 45 YALE L. J. 1339, 1340–1346; Henderson, *Statistical Activities of Trade Associations* (1926) 16 AM. EC. REV. SUPP. 219; Holbrook, *Price Reporting as a Trade Association Activity, 1925 to 1935* (1935) 35 COL. L. REV. 1053; A. R. BURNS, THE DECLINE OF COMPETITION (1936) ch. 2; PEARCE and others, TRADE ASSOCIATION SURVEY, TNEC MONOGRAPH No. 18 (1941) chs. 4–6; S. WHITNEY, TRADE ASSOCIATIONS AND INDUSTRIAL CONTROL (1934).

54. TNEC HEARINGS, Part 17, 9587–9593; COLE COMMITTEE HEARINGS, 148–197. See National Resources Committee, Energy Resources and National Policy (1939) 401–404.

55. See note 31 *supra*.

The Bureau of Mines estimates are broken down by states, so that they supply the state control agencies with an estimate of the potential market demand for crude from each state. This service, we are told by the chief economist of the Bureau of Mines, is "the primary purpose of the whole thing." [56] The state control agencies use these figures as the basis of their quotas of allowable production for the wells of the state. Sometimes they go a little above or a little below the Bureau of Mines figure, but generally they accept the quotas allotted to them by the federal agency. In most oil states, production control is accomplished by prorationing laws—laws which require or permit a state agency to fix the amount which each well can produce.[57] California achieves the same result, in bland defiance of the Anti-Trust laws, by a committee of the industry which operates to limit production to a monthly state quota, and to divide the quota among the wells of the state.[58] In Illinois no prorationing controls are in effect, but the amount of oil the Illinois wells can produce is so small that its effect on the structure of prices, and on the production of other states, has safely been ignored. There was a precarious moment or two, during 1940, when Illinois production rose to 145 million barrels, but in 1944 its production was 77 million barrels, less than 5 per cent, and the trend has been steadily downwards.[59]

56. TNEC HEARINGS, Part 17, 9591. See WATKINS, 106–119; COMPACT COMMISSION, Statistical Bulletins (1946). On the organization of the Department of the Interior with respect to oil matters, see O'MAHONEY HEARINGS, *Oil and Gas Division of the Department of the Interior* (1946) 6, 19–20.

57. Federal Oil Conservation Board, Ely (ed.), The Oil and Gas Conservation Statutes, Ann. (1933); Poe, *A Compendium of the State Gas Conservation Laws* (1945) 4 COMPACT COMMISSION BULL. (No. 1 and 2) 66; Wilson, *Louisiana's Oil and Gas Conservation Laws* (1944) 3 *id.* (No. 1) 13; Note (1946) 59 HARV. L. REV. 1142.

58. 1 and 2 BAIN; WATKINS, ch. 13; United States House of Representatives, *loc. cit. supra* note 50, 75–76; United States House of Representatives, Committee on Interstate and Foreign Commerce, Hearings on H. R. 9676 and H. R. 8572, 73d Cong., 2d Sess., *Oil and Oil Pipe Lines* (1934) 107–118; Federal Trade Commission, Report on the Pacific Coast Petroleum Industry, Parts I and II (1921); United States Department of Interior, Final Report, Marketing Division, Petroleum Administrative Board (1936) Part III.

59. United States, Bureau of Mines, Minerals Yearbook 1944 (1946) 1116; O'MAHONEY HEARINGS, *The Independent Petroleum Company* (1946) 409; COLE

The problems of law and policy presented by this extraordinary scheme of production control have been dealt with obliquely by the courts and legislatures. The Bureau of Mines estimates, the keystone of the entire plan, are without support in substantive legislation. No statute prescribes standards or policies for guiding the agency in its determinations of permissible supply. Presumably the Bureau of Mines appropriation items would be subject to a point of order, on the ground that the funds are being devoted to purposes unauthorized by law. The only statute at all in point is the Connally Act, which prohibits the shipment in interstate commerce of oil produced in violation of state conservation laws. The only semblance of a policy guide in the Connally Act is the vague proviso of Section 4, which permits the President to suspend its effect when he finds state restrictions so extreme as to cause "a lack of parity" between supply and demand.

So far as the state prorationing statutes are concerned, the Supreme Court has said a good deal without confronting the central fact that the statutes are part of a wide plan for controlling production. When in 1932, the Oklahoma prorationing law came before the Court, Mr. Justice Butler, for a unanimous bench, upheld the law against an attack on it as a confiscation, a price control plan, and an interference with interstate commerce. Mr. Justice Butler assimilated the problem presented by the statute to the earlier cases upholding laws regulating the methods of oil extraction. The issue, and the only substantial issue, he said, was conservation, or the prevention of waste. The premise on which the *Champlin* case rests is that limiting production, and prorationing the total of allowable production among the wells of the state, is constitutional *because* it constitutes a conservation device, and a method of preventing the physical waste of petroleum.[60]

The premise is entirely untenable. The contribution which the prorationing statutes make to the cause of conservation is

COMMITTEE HEARINGS, 169 *ff.*; Comment, *The Need for Oil Conservation in Illinois* (1940) 35 ILL. L. REV. 175; ILL. REV. STAT. (1945) ch. 104, §§ 62–88.

60. Champlin Refining Co. v. Corporation Commission of Oklahoma, 286 U. S. 210 (1932).

incidental and secondary. Their chief effect on conservation policy is to prohibit flush operations of the gusher type, a prohibition which would be available either separately or under any alternative form of regulation.

One should distinguish at least two conceptions of waste in this connection. From the geologist's point of view, waste is any procedure which reduces the ultimate extraction of oil from the underground reservoir. The geologist's idea of good policy is simple—he is interested in maximum total recovery through time. He makes no distinction between the present and the future. A barrel of oil tomorrow is worth as much to him as a barrel today. The economist, on the other hand, talks of waste in an altogether different sense. To him waste is production which it would pay to postpone or forego. In this sense, restricting production would pay the community if the discounted expected value of future barrels of oil were greater than the present value of additional oil. Oil can be produced in a number of alternative ways, and at various alternative rates. The geologist would be interested in the plan of production which yielded the maximum total volume through time, the economist in the procedure for producing oil at the rate which would maximize the present discounted value of the total flow of production through time. Geologically sound methods of extraction are almost invariably slower than the quick cheap procedure of utilizing gusher and open-flow methods in flush pools. The economist would approve postponement of use, or limitation of production, only if in terms of this concept it paid to do so.[61]

61. WATKINS, ch. 4; Rostow, *Bituminous Coal and the Public Interest* (1941) 50 YALE L. J. 543, 548–553, 571–573; KEMNITZER, REBIRTH OF MONOPOLY (1938) chs. 8, 10; O'MAHONEY HEARINGS, *Investigation of Petroleum Resources*, 78–92, 128–135, 289–317; TNEC HEARINGS, Part 14, 7112–7143, 7435–7491 (testimony of Dr. Joseph Pogue); 7389–7423 (testimony of E. De Golyer); Part 15, 8206–8249 (testimony of E. O. Thompson); Part 17, 9796–9809; COLE COMMITTEE HEARINGS, 534–535. S. v. Ciriacy-Wantrup [*Taxation and the Conservation of Resources* (1944) 58 Q. J. ECON. 157] states the goal of conservation policy from the economic point of view as the maximization of the present value of net revenues, giving full discount to expected future values (164–167).

The difficulty with the problem is the unpredictability of the future. The literature about the extent of oil reserves is full of apparent controversy, the optimistic experts claiming that there is no chance of an oil shortage, the pessimists that a shortage at least of cheap oil is upon us.

These seem to be the main propositions of the debate.

If we seriously contemplate importing petroleum products —and from the point of view of national defense that would seem a prudent course in peace time—there is little or no risk of our lacking low-cost oils for the significant future. Known reserves in South America, the Middle East and other areas of the world are very large indeed.[62]

As for the domestic oil supply situation, liquid fuels are now chiefly produced from crude oil. They could also be produced from oil shale, which exists in large deposits; from bituminous coal, of which our reserves are huge; or from natural gas, of which the reserve supply is probably also ample. So far as crude oil itself is concerned, one must distinguish between reserves which have already been proved, tested, and approximately measured, and areas where there is a reasonable geological expectation of finding oil. Except for the period immediately before the war, the rate of discovery of proven reserves has for twenty years or more been steadily equal to or greater than our annual consumption of oil, great as that has been, both because of the identification of new fields, and because of improvements in techniques of drilling and extraction. We are accustomed to hear statistics about the number of years' supply known to be in proved reserve. That figure at the end of 1944 stood at about 12 years' supply at present high rates of consumption. The paradox is that in 1936, the estimate

62. The most recent material on reserves, and on sources of liquid fuel, appear in the O'MAHONEY HEARINGS, *Investigation of Petroleum Resources* (1945), *passim*, and *Petroleum Requirements—Postwar* (1946) 43-76; and in the COLE COMMITTEE HEARINGS, *passim*; United States Tariff Commission, War Changes in Industry Series, Report No. 17, Petroleum (1946); B. I. BROOKS, PEACE, PLENTY AND PETROLEUM (1944); W. PRATT, OIL IN THE EARTH (1943); *id.*, THERE WILL BE ENOUGH OIL (1944); *id., Our Petroleum Resources* (1944) 32 AMERICAN SCIENTIST 120; FANNING (ed.), OUR OIL RESOURCES (1945) chs. 5-8.

was that only 10 years' supply, at a much lower rate of consumption, was then in sight. Alarmist conclusions from such simplified statistics are entirely unjustified.[63]

One can guess at the magnitude of the discovery problem by some crude arithmetic of this order: the area of the United States is about 3 million square miles. About 50 per cent of that area, or 1½ million square miles, is classified by geologists as likely to contain oil. Known oil reserves now exist in an area of only 8,000 square miles. In short, we now know the oil possibilities of about ½₀₀ of the area which the geologists say is likely to contain oil.[64] Moreover, the application of deeper drilling methods is altering our estimates of the amounts recoverable from fields now known, and the use of offshore oil, now in its infancy in the United States, will in all likelihood turn the present statistics about future oil supply upside down.

An even more spectacular situation exists for natural gas. Our estimates of gas reserves have jumped from 15 trillion cubic feet in 1919 to 70 trillions in 1939, and over 140 in 1945. Meanwhile, the consumption of natural gas for all purposes—carbon black, direct use as fuel, and as the basic raw material for making gasoline, formaldehyde, alcohols, ketones, etc.—has gone up tremendously.[65]

While our potential domestic resources in liquid fuel continue to grow, and there is every reason to suppose that the process of growth will continue, although perhaps at higher levels of cost, the future uses of liquid fuels become more problematical. Other forms of energy are pushing into sight, and the technology of using coal and its derivatives, both directly and as a source of liquid fuel, has been improved. The oil industry now thinks that it will outstrip our existing chemical industry in the field of synthetics, and some bulk chem-

63. O'MAHONEY HEARINGS, *Investigation of Petroleum Resources* (1945) 40; see also 4–54, 275–281.

64. *Id.*, 48–49.

65. *Id.*, 54–58, 320–322, 89–91, 120–135; Symposium (1942) 1 COMPACT COMMISSION BULL. (No. 3) 7–98; Stephenson, *Natural Gas and Post-War Period* (1943) 2 COMPACT COMMISSION BULL. (No. 3) 33; Symposium (1945) 4 COMPACT COMMISSION BULL. (No. 1 and 2) 4–211.

icals. That remains to be seen. At the same time, the technology of war is changing so fast that many of the traditional military justifications for the scale of the domestic oil industry may be radically altered.

Both the optimists and the pessimists among the experts seem to agree that while we have only 15 years' or so supply of crude oil in clear sight at any moment, we have enough reserves of liquid fuel, or will find them, for the indefinite future. One might reasonably anticipate that the future costs of producing liquid fuel by methods now orthodox will go up. Nonetheless, it is not possible to infer from this any long-term rise in the price of gasoline, since technological progress has in the past steadily exerted a downward pressure on prices. So the process of determining the present value of a future barrel of American crude becomes inscrutable and insoluble, except in terms of the broad proposition that no radical increase in real costs seem likely.

There is enough doubt about such predictions, however, to make some forms of physical "waste" in the production of oil worth preventing. People prefer at least to believe that they are on the safe side; and besides, it is emotionally very difficult to be against conservation. If we were really serious about conserving our oil supply, we would eliminate our oil tariffs; we would use foreign oil in peace time, and perhaps have a holiday in one or more areas of production, keeping the American oil extraction industry as a model plant, and a standby for defense purposes; we would mix gasoline with alcohol made from grain; and we would discourage consumption by a horse-power tax, and perhaps by a prohibition against using oil where coal or water power would do. But we are not really serious about oil conservation, and there isn't much objective ground for urging that we should be. However, our public policy is loyal indeed to the slogan of conservation. It is the supposed objective of our production control system, as it is the moving idea which has persuaded the Supreme Court and the public to condone our present monopoly methods of determining supply.

CHAPTER 5

Prorationing and Conservation

In actual practice, our present system of production controls can make little or no contribution to the goals of a conservation program.

From the geologist's point of view, the best utilization of the energy potential of each reservoir requires that methods of production take full account of the geological peculiarities of that field. There is no such thing as an engineering optimum rate of production for all fields, or for all wells. So-called distillate or condensate fields require one technique for technologically efficient operation, in which reservoir pressure is maintained above the level at which condensation takes place (otherwise a large part of the condensed liquids becomes unrecoverable by present techniques); water pressure and gas pressure fields require an adaptation of drilling procedures to the structure of the field, particularly by the location of wells within the field, and their respective rates of operation.

Although there is controversy as to each of these propositions, the geological criteria of good recovery practice may be summed up in these broad terms: (1) there should be no flush flows: that is, the rush of oil and gas when a pool is first opened leads to a loss of gas pressure, and a possible reduction of ultimate recoveries without the use of secondary extraction techniques; (2) the number of wells on a field should be at a minimum: each well inevitably loses some gas pressure. The number of wells on the field should be determined by the geological character of the field. If there are too few wells, oil will be lost during the migration of the oil from its location underground to the well point. If there are too many wells, gas or water pressure will be needlessly lost in the process of extraction. The optimum minimum number of wells for any field cannot be determined by any rule of thumb—so many wells per acre.

It may be appropriate geologically to have three or more wells on some acres over the reservoir, and none at all on others, depending on the formations beneath. (3) Thirdly, the flow from each well should be at a rate which equalizes the rate of change of pressure throughout the field. That is, the ratio of pressure at the well head to pressure at the well foot should be approximately the same for all wells. Thus the rate of flow throughout the field would be uniform, and the loss of ultimate recovery through unnecessary migration from an area of slow flow to an area of rapid flow would be minimized. (4) Finally, the best guide for pinching each well seems to be the minimal ratio of gas to oil at which there will be a flow from the well. Such practice would extract the oil by using a minimal number of cubic feet of gas per barrel of crude, and avoid the physical waste which arises when the rate of flow is too slow to permit oil to emerge at all.[66]

The common characteristic of these principles, except for the first one, is that they vary in their application to each part of an oil field and to each well in an oil field. Their application depends on the geological structure of the field, and the relation of its wells to each other.

The prevailing system of production control prohibits flush flows, but otherwise violates all the geologists' rules of conservation practice.

In the first place, the basic and dominant purpose of our present methods of production control is to limit production to what the Bureau of Mines estimates will be market demand, at a price. There is no reason to suppose that "market demand at a price" corresponds to the amount which at any time would represent the geologist's optimum rate of withdrawal from oil reservoirs.[67] On the contrary, as new fields are discovered and

66. See note 61 *supra*, and STOCKING, THE OIL INDUSTRY AND THE COMPETITIVE SYSTEM (1925) chs. 8–10; O'MAHONEY HEARINGS, *Investigation of Petroleum Resources* (1945) 78–92, 107–115; *id., War-time Petroleum Policy under the P. A. W.* (1945) 73–76, 87; DE GOLYER (ed.), TRANSACTIONS OF THE AMERICAN INSTITUTE OF MECHANICAL AND MINING ENGINEERS (1930); Lovejoy, *Production Technology* in FANNING (ed.), OUR OIL RESOURCES (1945) 80–98.

67. See POGUE, ECONOMICS OF THE PETROLEUM INDUSTRY (1939) 22–24; TNEC HEARINGS, Part 17, 9949 (testimony of W. S. Farish).

new methods of extraction employed, the geologist's norm of optimum recovery must change in proportion. The optimum rate of withdrawal from a larger known oil reserve must as a matter of arithmetic be a larger amount.

Secondly, our present system of controls does not keep the number of wells to a minimum. It is true that in most states there are well-spacing statutes or regulations, as there are for the federal domain, limiting the capacity of surface owners to drill except at a rate of so many wells per acre, and further limiting their capacity to drill offset wells, near the boundaries of their tracts. But such regulations do not meet the conservation problem. The formation of a pool may make one well per acre wasteful in one area, and insufficient in another. Moreover, the well-spacing regulations are honored largely in the breach. It is the practice to grant exceptions to the regulations freely. A state regulatory body would be hard put to it to refuse such exceptions, which may be the only way to permit the owner of a small surface tract his individual chance to reach oil. Since each surface owner hopes to strike an East Texas field under his backyard or woodlot, it would be difficult for a state agency to resist the pressure. In the *Rowan & Nichols* cases, for example, in which the fairness of a prorationing formula was under constitutional review, the trial court found as a fact that the field could have been operated efficiently with 10,000 wells, whereas there were over 25,000 wells in production.[68]

The reason is not hard to find. The pattern of control policy presented in the *Rowan & Nichols* cases is one designed to stimulate drilling on a large scale. The complainants in those cases were seeking to enjoin the enforcement of an order of

68. Railroad Commission v. Rowan & Nichols Oil Co., 310 U. S. 573 (1940), 311 U. S. 570, 614 (1941), Record on Appeal in 311 U. S. 570, at 544 (fol. 756). More than 65 per cent of the wells in the field were completed as exceptions to the well-spacing regulations. *Id.*, 540 (fol. 751). See also Burford v. Sun Oil Co., 319 U. S. 315 (1943).

See Summers, *Does the Regulation of Oil Production Require the Denial of Due Process and the Equal Protection of the Laws?* (1940) 19 Tex. L. Rev. 1; Summers, *The Rowan & Nichols Cases* (1941) 13 Miss. L. J. 417; Comment (1942) 51 Yale L. J. 680. Note also Pogue, Economics of the Petroleum Industry (1939) 26–27. And see note 35 *supra* and note 76 *infra*.

the Texas Railroad Commission restricting their production to about 2 per cent of their capacity at open flow. The total allowable for the field was 522,000 barrels a day, in the first of the two cases, and 691,000 barrels a day in the second. There was no consideration in the opinions of the propriety of the total allowables, nor of the basis on which they were fixed. The only question discussed was the fairness of the division of the quota among the wells of the field. The Commission had divided the wells into three classes. The first class consisted of those which were incapable of producing 20 barrels a day at full open flow. There were between 400 and 500 such wells, and they were allowed to produce all they could. The bulk of the wells on the field, about 20,000 in number, came in a second class—those which could not produce 20 barrels a day at the proration fraction, which happened to be 2.32 per cent of their total capacity. These wells were allowed to produce a minimal figure of 20 barrels a day. The other wells on the field, approximately 6,000 of the best and most productive wells, were allowed to produce an equal fraction of their potential until the remainder of the quota for the field was exhausted. In the first case, this meant that the complainants' seven wells could produce a little more than 22 barrels a day, and in the second case about 37 barrels. In the first case, over 98 per cent of the field's quota was absorbed in the flat per well allowances; in the second case, about 75 per cent.

The difference between the Railroad Commission's procedure in the two cases is worth noting. In the first case a lower court injunction was obtained on the ground, in considerable part, that the Commission in rationing the allowable had not given enough consideration to the quality of the properties in different parts of the field. It asserted as a rule of constitutional law that the right of a surface owner to oil had to be measured with reference to the amount of oil supposed to be "in place" under his property: a persistent survival of the idea that a man "owns" the oil beneath his Blackacre. In order to carry on the process of regulation pending the appeal, the Commission changed its nominal formula, supposedly taking into account the bottom hole pressure, and the quality of the underlying oil sands, as well as the total hourly potential production of the wells on the field. It then shook up its figures and came out with much the same result as before, the bulk of the allowable going in flat allowances per well.

The Supreme Court of the United States upheld both orders, on the ground that it had no constitutional right to interfere in an expert administrative body's choice between various methods of dividing the pie. In other cases, it has gone so far as to suggest that a claim of unfairness under such circumstances presented no constitutional, or other federal, question, but raised only the question whether the state agency had complied with the applicable provisions of the state law—an issue, it has been suggested, which can be tried only in the state courts, even in cases where the parties are citizens of different states.[69]

These cases raise intriguing questions as to the present status of substantive due process, and the freedom of federal and state administrative bodies to find their own rules of economic control policy. Since the possibility of treating the entire production control plan as an obstruction to and a burden upon interstate commerce was not raised, the appeal was confined to the issue of unfairness or confiscation. So far as the *Rowan & Nichols* cases are concerned, the surface owner's "property" in the subsurface oil is not what he can capture, nor yet a claim to the oil "in place" beneath his tract; he has an ownership interest in whatever oil the state through its regulatory agencies allows him to withdraw. Since no one is supposed to have a "vested" right in a rule of law, even a rule of property law, the result in these terms is neither surprising nor very shocking. Nonetheless, the older premise about the oil a surface owner might claim has been extremely persistent, and may not be quite dead, despite the *Rowan & Nichols* cases. That rule might be put in these terms: the surface owner can

---

69. Burford v. Sun Oil Co., 319 U. S. 315 (1943). And see Patterson v. Stanolind Oil & Gas Co., 305 U. S. 376 (1939). *Cf.* Hunter Co. v. McHugh, 320 U. S. 222 (1943); Comment (1942) 51 YALE L. J. 680.

withdraw whatever oil will rise through a well drilled on his surface land, subject to state regulations in the interest of conservation policy, or of assuring a fair division of the underground oil among the surface owners.

The older premise finds its most forceful expression in Mr. Justice Brandeis' opinion for a unanimous court in the *Thompson* case.[70] The *Thompson* case concerned an order prorationing the allowable production of natural gas, substantially identical with the orders under review in the *Rowan & Nichols* cases. Mr. Justice Brandeis said that "our law reports present no more glaring instance of the taking of one man's property and giving it to another." [71] The order, he said, did not serve conservation purposes, despite contrary findings of fact by the administrative agency which issued it, and in his view was therefore an unconstitutional limitation on the complainant's freedom to use his property for business purposes. The order was invalid because it had in fact the purpose of forcing a gas producer who owned a pipe line to restrict his production, in order to provide an outlet for the production of non-integrated producers. Such producers could not transport their gas to the market without using the complainant's pipe line. If they did not produce, while the complainant did, they might lose all their potential production, by underground migration. If they did so produce, they would have difficulty in shipping, selling or storing the gas, and might therefore be forced to let it escape. In the *Rowan & Nichols* cases too, complainants could and did assert that they could themselves use more than the oil they were allowed to produce. They could say, as Mr. Justice Brandeis said of the plaintiffs in the *Thompson* case, that their own "operations are neither causing nor threatening any overground or underground waste"; that the proration order reduces their allowable production "to a volume far below *their* requirements," and "could not prevent waste *attributable to them*" (italics added).[72]

70. Thompson v. Consolidated Gas Utilities Corp., 300 U. S. 55 (1937).
71. *Id.*, 79–80.
72. *Id.*, 77, 66, 72.

But Mr. Justice Frankfurter was not concerned with the controversy as to whether the prorationing orders did or did not serve a conservation purpose. He refused to take sides in "a conflict of expertise." [73] Whether the Railroad Commission of Texas complied with the standards of the state statute in establishing its prorationing system was a question of state, not of federal law. The due process clause of the Fourteenth Amendment was not a sanction generally available to ensure that state courts interpreted state statutes in ways which appealed to the Supreme Court.

There was a possible federal question in the prorationing controversy which neither litigant, nor the courts, discussed. The Interstate Oil Compact, to which Texas was a party, provides that "it is not the purpose of this compact to authorize the states joining herein to limit the production of oil or gas for the purpose of stabilizing or fixing the price thereof, or create or perpetuate monopoly, or to promote regimentation, but is limited to the purpose of conserving oil and gas and preventing the avoidable waste thereof within reasonable limitations." [74] Congress gave its consent to the Compact, as it must under Article I, Section 10 of the Constitution, in order to give it the force of law. By that Compact, Texas has agreed with its co-signatory states, and with the Congress, to enact conservation legislation for specified purposes, and committed itself not to enact legislation which has for its purpose price control, monopoly or "regimentation." Whether the legislation in question complied with the standards of the Compact was a problem of policy for interstate commerce in which the Congress had a great and overriding interest. In all probability, it presents a federal question, which the federal courts are required to consider.[75]

73. 310 U. S. 573, 582 (1940).
74. 57 Stat. 383, 385 (1943). See Frey, *The Interstate Oil Compact*, in National Resources Committee, Energy Resources and National Policy (1939) 397.
75. See Hinderlider v. La Plata River & Cherry Creek Ditch Co., 304 U. S. 92 (1938). Apart from the issue, raised by dictum in the *Hinderlider* case, as to the effect of Congressional approval of the compact on federal jurisdiction (see 304 U. S. at 109), there is the basic federal issue of the effect of the compact and the underlying Texas statute on interstate commerce. See note 177 *infra*.

Apart from the question of the scope of the court's review of administrative orders in the field of oil production, the policy represented in the *Rowan & Nichols* cases is an extraordinary departure from canons of conservation practice. It employs the technique of rationing the quota of limited production among the oil producers largely by allowing each well a fixed minimal allowance of 20 barrels' production a day. This is a practice which has no possible justification from the point of view of conservation. The geologists look at the field as a whole, and want it run as a unit, with each well producing an appropriate amount, which would inevitably be different for each well, so as best to utilize the variable pressure resources of the reservoir. Instead of minimizing the number of wells, the policy of the *Rowan & Nichols* cases sets up an irresistible demand for more wells. If each well is entitled at the worst to 20 barrels a day, then the prudent course for a surface owner to follow is to dig more and more wells. While it is highly economic for the individual oil producer under such a rule to put down additional wells, it is utter waste for society as a whole. The extra wells represent an additional cost which does not result in increasing output or potential output. In fact, by providing another outlet for the limited gas energy of the pool, it probably will reduce the ultimate oil potential of the field. A considerable fraction of such wells are surely redundant, except in terms of prorationing procedures. An authoritative estimate puts the cost of unnecessary wells at nearly $100,000-000 a year, and their number near 4,000 to 5,000. This cost is equal to a gross production tax of nearly 10 cents a barrel for every barrel produced. These figures almost certainly understate the problem.[76]

Moreover, the impact of prorationing as a production control technique is to prevent an economic allocation and use of

76. See COLE COMMITTEE HEARINGS, 352–358; Ely, *The Conservation of Oil* (1938) 51 HARV. L. REV. 1209. ("Defects in the control of drilling constitute the heaviest indictment against the conservation system at its present stage," p. 1230). As to the effect of prorationing orders on well drilling, see note 68 *supra*, and Railroad Commission v. Rowan & Nichols Oil Co., 310 U. S. 573 (1940), Record on Appeal, 973–976.

resources, and to perpetuate an expensive one. A government-controlled rationing system, unlike the rationing device of market price, must give everyone a chance. The kind of controls represented in the *Rowan & Nichols* cases assure all producers, high and low cost alike, a share in the market. Quite apart from the effect of prorationing on the size of the total supply, and on the volume of expenditures for steel, other equipment and labor in drilling, prorationing prevents the full use of lower cost resources, and thus imposes an additional and serious tax on society.[77]

77. See WATKINS, 125 *ff.*, for some examples. As to the differences in production costs as between wells and fields, see United States, Department of the Interior, Petroleum Administrative Board, Report on the Cost of Producing Crude Petroleum (1936); United States Tariff Commission, Report on the Cost of Producing Crude Petroleum (1942) 53 ("Proration and the regulation of oil field development . . . have tended . . . to result in higher immediate costs of production.")

CHAPTER 6

Conservation, Unitization, and the Limitation of Supply to "Demand"

THERE are other aspects of the controversy over conservation policy which require consideration.

The first, and simplest, is the argument which satisfied Mr. Justice Butler in the *Champlin* case. Limitation of production to market demand, he argued, is a way to prevent the physical waste of petroleum.[78] If people produce more than the "market demand" for petroleum products, they will be unable to sell the product, and will therefore store the crude as best they can. Storage in steel tanks is expensive and not generally available. And storage in ditches on the surface of the earth is risky, since the oil may evaporate, seep away or catch fire. The difficulty with the argument is its assumption that the Bureau of Mines estimates of market demand are sacred, and that anything produced beyond that amount could not be sold by means of price adjustment. Practical experience in all phases of the oil industry daily confirms the fact that prices are readily adjusted to local problems of supply, and that the market is commonly cleared, in the event of a temporary glut, by price reduction.

In more sophisticated forms, Mr. Justice Butler's argument reappears in many contexts.[79] The geology of oil, it is contended, and the existing law of real property with respect to oil, are such as to make an over-all limitation of production es-

78. Champlin Refining Co. v. Corporation Commission of Oklahoma, 286 U. S. 210, 230–231 (1932).

79. WATKINS, 38–39; SHUMAN, THE PETROLEUM INDUSTRY (1940) 250–282; Ely, *The Conservation of Oil* (1938) 51 HARV. L. REV. 1209; TNEC HEARINGS, Part 17, 9946–9949; National Resources Committee, Energy Resources and National Policy (1939) 186–200; O'MAHONEY HEARINGS, *Investigation of Petroleum Resources* (1945) 78–82, 128–135; Note (1946) 59 HARV. L. REV. 1142, 1145. And see Marshall and Meyers, *Legal Planning of Petroleum Production* (1931) 41 YALE L. J. 33 (1933) 42 *id.* 702, 707–740, and note P. H. FRANKEL, ESSENTIALS OF PETROLEUM (1946) 23 *ff.* (overhead costs).

sential in the interest of preventing both physical waste, and the destruction of all capital values in oil property. The thesis runs along these lines: that offset drilling is a necessity on a large scale to prevent capital losses through the drainage and migration of underground oil; that the whole of the potential supply of oil is "surplus" overhanging the market; and that in the absence of a limit on production, the pressure for what is called "over-production" would therefore be irresistible. On the side of conservation, this argument is concerned with the economic effects of the rule of capture. Wouldn't the desire to prevent a neighbor from draining away one's total potential production lead to production that could not be sold at any price, and would therefore be stored as effectively as possible, so that a fraction could be saved rather than to have the total supply lost to a neighbor producer? The mass surface storage of oil is bound to be either prohibitively expensive or to lead to physical loss of the product. Therefore, the argument runs, limitations of production are necessary to prevent physical waste.

The phenomenon of physical waste through storage above ground, which made such a vivid impression on the courts as a justification for prorationing controls, has been a limited and occasional experience in the industry, largely confined to the depression of the early thirties. In assessing the potential importance of such wastes in storage, induced by the possibility of capital losses through the offset drilling of others, one must weigh the fact that even without benefit of the over-all limitations of production established during the last fifteen years or so, all wells did not operate 24 hours a day during the earlier history of the industry, and that the total of production did fall from time to time, as demand fell. In short, market forces did operate to determine the level of output even under the regime of the rule of capture, perhaps irregularly because of offset drilling and like pressures, but nonetheless effectively, except where the problem of adjusting production to market pressures was complicated by the discovery of great new fields, whose appearance completely altered the supply position of the market.

Should the irregularities in market response associated with the rule of capture be controlled, and if so, how? The author is one of those who have come to the conclusion that the rule of capture has proved, for this perhaps among other reasons, a socially undesirable rule of law, and that it should be changed as the root idea of our system of oil law. The preferable way to change it, however, is to impose unitary operations on the fields, rather than to undertake further experiments with the cumbersome, expensive and unsatisfactory plan of prorationing. The compulsory operation of all fields as units of production could be accomplished by requiring the organization of companies or cooperatives in which all surface owners would share on an equitable basis, either in proportion to their surface ownership or to the richness of underlying deposits. Oil production under such units could altogether eliminate the possible wastes associated with offset drilling and the other consequences of the rule of capture, as well as the many geologists' criticisms of the administration of prorationing laws. It would for the first time permit the number of wells to be kept to a minimum, and the flow from individual wells on the field to be determined by geological criteria rather than the accidental pattern of ownership of the land over the oil. The unitary operation of the oil fields is the only course of action which as a practical matter could permit high standards of conservation practice to be seriously followed.[80]

80. Compulsory or voluntary unitization has long been urged as a conservation device. It is the rule in many foreign oil fields, and is permitted and encouraged, and now may be required, on the federal domain. 46 STAT. 1007, 1523, 1524 (1930) (1931), 49 STAT. 674, 677 (1935), 30 U. S. C. §§ 184, 226 (1940); COLE COMMITTEE HEARINGS, 409–440; United States Senate, Subcommittee of the Committee on Public Lands and Surveys, Hearings on S. 1236, *Development of Oil and Gas on the Public Domain*, 79th Cong., 1st Sess. (1945), Parts I and II. Recent statutes in Louisiana [LA. GEN. STAT. (Dart. Supp. 1946) § 4741.19] and in Oklahoma [OKLA. STAT. (Cum. Supp. 1946) tit. 52, § 87] authorize administrative agencies under certain circumstances to require unitization. They have not yet, however, been widely applied except on a voluntary basis. Unitization is undoubtedly constitutional, Marrs v. City of Oxford, 32 F. (2d) 134 (C.C.A.

Many students of the oil problem agree that unitary operation of the oil fields would be desirable, from the conservation point of view, but believe that even if unitization were adopted, an over-all limitation of production to "market demand" would be required, in order to prevent the physical wastes associated with "over-production." Professor Bain has formulated a typical statement of the theory underlying this contention:

Since the large California discoveries of the period subsequent to 1917, and more particularly since the great discoveries in east Texas, the United States has had a great potential "surplus" of crude petroleum. The term "surplus" is used advisedly—to indicate a condition where the potential crude production was greatly in excess of domestic needs (except at prices far below those prevailing before the great new discoveries), and where unrestricted production would therefore drive the price of crude to very low levels (perhaps approximating the direct cost of extraction). The probable results of such unrestricted production would therefore be: (1), a very low domestic price of crude, together with greatly increased export of domestic oil reserves; (2), a destruction of the preexisting investment values in crude properties and facilities based on the prices of crude antedating the new discoveries; (3), a rapid rate of use of existing oil reserves, including uses of low economic value; (4), an unstable price situation for crude and for refined products, because of supply varying irregularly in accordance with variations in the unrestricted rate of flow of oil; and

8th, 1929), *cert. denied* 280 U. S. 573 (1929); and cases cited in note 69 *supra,* which arose under the statutes mentioned above. And unitization has been vigorously supported on engineering grounds. United States House of Representatives, Committee on Interstate and Foreign Commerce, Hearings on H. Res. 441, 73d Cong. (Recess) (1934) Part 2, 1249–1273; COLE COMMITTEE HEARINGS, 391–399, 409–440; O'MAHONEY HEARINGS, *Investigation of Petroleum Resources* (1945) 87–88, 97, 227, 416–418, 443–445; Comment (1945) 45 YALE L. J. 324, 333; Gibson, *Scientific Unit Control,* in A. DUNSTAN and others, THE SCIENCE OF PETROLEUM (1938) vol. 1, 534–540 (valuable bibliography); German, *Compulsory Unit Operation of Oil Pools* (1931) 17 A. B. A. J. 393, (1932) 20 CALIF. L. REV. 111; Ford, *Controlling the Production of Oil* (1932) 30 MICH. L. REV. 1170; Note (1942) 16 TULANE L. REV. 477; National Resources Committee, Energy Resources and National Policy (1939) 199.

. It has been suggested that ambiguity as to the income tax status of groups organized to operate unitization programs is a major deterrent to their development.

(5), subsurface loss of oil reserves due to uneconomical use of gas pressure under the ground and to the fact that stripper-well production would be discouraged by a low price.

To the word "ground" in the last sentence, Professor Bain added this footnote: "The natural gas pressure will force more oil in total to the surface if the flow is stemmed to some degree." [81]

This statement, which Professor Bain regards as presenting the reasons why "the public may very properly be interested in restricting the rate of use of oil reserves," is not intended to distinguish between prorationing and unitization as possible alternative methods of regulating the production of oil. Professor Bain points out that in fact "the two objectives of conservation and of limitation of competition, in the crude market and above it, are inextricably compounded." He expressly refuses "to argue the specific merits of limitation of production in general or of various degrees of limitation in particular." [82]

The reasons advanced by Professor Bain would, if tenable, justify limitations on output even though all the geologists' rules of conservation practice were enforced as part of a regime of unitization. His view is that the "surplus," or more exactly, the existing reserves of oil, are so large as to justify control of supply in order to keep prices at or about the prevailing or customary level, and thus preserve the value of investments. [83]

The first problem presented by this contention is the effect of unutilized capacity on supply and on production. There are at any moment approximately 12 to 15 years' supply of crude oil in clear sight. Not all the potential production from proved reserves could be produced in any one year, even if all restric-

81. 1 BAIN, 60.
82. *Id.*, 61. See Loftus, Review (1945) 35 AM. EC. REV. 727, and Bain, Reply (1946) 36 AM. EC. REV. 148.
83. Part of Professor Bain's case for preventing the price of petroleum products from falling seems to rest on the view that lower prices would encourage the export of oil products, and their use in place of other sources of energy, to be deplored from the point of view of conservation. One would suppose that a direct approach to such problems would be more effective than a policy of keeping prices up. See *supra*, p. 33.

tions on output were removed. If all the wells and all the refineries were worked all day and all night, seven days a week, total production would be greater than it is, but, as we found out during the war, it would not equal the total supply refined in 15 average years.

In the absence of over-all limitations on supply, what market pressures would arise from the presence of known oil reserves? The problem is not unique to the oil industry. There are comparable known reserves of coal, iron ore, lumber, copper, and, indeed, of all minerals and many other natural products. Somehow or other in all these markets the decision is made as to how much of potential supply will be produced in any one year. Neither in the oil industry, during its unregulated period, nor in other comparable industries, does the existence of reserves have the effect which Professor Bain assumes would occur in the absence of rules restricting production to total estimated demand. The existence of unused capacity does not seem regularly to keep production at its theoretical maximum, and prices below the level of profitability. The amount which it pays to produce is almost never the total of potential physical production. In 1926 refining capacity was not fully used, although it was a year of important crude oil discoveries, 62 per cent of independent capacity being employed, as compared with 49 per cent in 1937, and 81 per cent of major capacity, as compared with 85 per cent in 1937.[84] And the measure of refining capacity in itself has arbitrary elements, being based on estimates of the quantities of different refined products which might be produced under various hypothetical operating conditions. Before we had over-all limitations on output, production varied from year to year, and prices both rose and fell. Neither experience nor analysis support the view that even under a regime of unitization the production of oil would be carried forward to socially uncompensatory levels.[85]

84. Cook, 34 (twenty companies counted as majors).

85. See generally, Chamberlin, The Theory of Monopolistic Competition (5th ed. 1946); Hutt, The Theory of Idle Resources (1939); Caplan, *Premature Abandonment and the Flow of Investment* (1939) 54 Q. J. Econ. 152; Cassels, *Excess Capacity and Monopolistic Competition* (1937) 51 Q. J. Econ. 426; Kaldor, *Market Imperfection and Excess Capacity* (1935) 2 Economica (N. S.) 33; Reynolds, *Cutthroat Competition* (1940) 30 Am. Ec. Rev. 736; Rostow, *supra* note 61, 549 ff.

One's views depend on a greater particularization of what is meant by saying that prices are "too" low. Professor Bain contends that in the absence of limitations on production, the known reserves of oil would drive the price "to very low levels (perhaps approximating the direct cost of extraction)." So far as the economic pressures determining output are concerned, one would expect that output be carried forward until for each producer the additional revenue attributable to the last unit of his output equalled the additional costs it entailed. But such a determination of the level of output does not mean that prices would be unprofitable, or competition "destructive," especially if the risk of capital loss incident to present patterns of well ownership were eliminated under a system of unitization. Professor Bain's conclusion results from confusing the individual seller with the market as a whole, and marginal with average direct costs. For each producer under competitive conditions (the "producer" in this instance being the unitized field), marginal cost would equal marginal revenue and therefore price; but marginal cost for each producer might be at or above his average costs at that level of output. For the market as a whole price would not equal "the direct cost of extraction" (presumably Professor Bain means an average of such costs) for all producers, but only the direct costs of the producer, if there were any, at the margin of indecision as to whether to remain in production. Output for each seller would be determined by the relation of his costs to the level of market price, increments to output continuing to be profitable for each seller so long as his expected additional revenues exceed his additional costs. Thus for sellers at the margin of indecision, operations might be compensatory only in the sense that operating costs were being met, or operating losses minimized. But for the bulk of sellers, assuming a normal distribution between higher and lower cost producers, production should not be unprofitable unless demand falls off sharply (as during a depression), while costs remain fixed.[86] The remedy for that

86. See Machlup, *Marginal Analysis and Empirical Research* (1946) 36 AM. EC. REV. 519, 541 *ff.*; *id., Practical Significance of the Theory of Monopolistic Competition* (1939) 29 AM. EC. REV. 227; KAHN, *Some Notes on Ideal Output*

kind of unprofitability, however, is not monopoly restriction of output, but general measures of reflation calculated to restore the level of national income.[87]

It may be, on the other hand, that oil producing capacity has been built up by a regime of monopoly, or by the rate of discovery, to a point which makes its utilization under competitive conditions (even under a regime of unitization) likely to produce prices which will not yield a return on present capital investment, at least for higher cost fields. This conclusion seems unlikely, in view of the steady secular increase in the demand for petroleum products, and the fact that recent increases in proven reserves have largely been extensions of known fields, rather than discoveries of altogether new ones. Nonetheless, if it were the fact, it would simply be another way of saying that the competitive value of oil fields had fallen. It would hardly follow that the proper criterion for public policy should be to keep prices at a level which would maintain pre-existing investment values, and thus attract new investment into the field, to enlarge the supposed "excess" of capacity, and thus to make the alleged disease worse.

Professor Bain's argument sharply raises the question of what the purpose of oil control policy should be. His statement is peppered with undefined words of strong emotional connotation: prices are identified as "very low" and as "unstable," not as "competitive" or "flexible." [88] He frankly advances the view that production controls are justifiable in order to validate investments made in anticipation of the continu-

---

(1935) 45 Econ. J. 1. See A. R. Burns, The Decline of Competition (1936) 542 ff. As to cost conditions, consider the studies of the U. S. Tariff Commission, Report on the Cost of Producing Crude Petroleum in the United States (1942), Supplemental Report (1943); 2 Bain, *passim*.

87. See Pigou, *Stabilization in Particular Industries* (1927) in Pigou and Robertson, Economic Essays and Addresses (1931) 34; L. Robbins, The Economic Basis of Class Conflict (1939); Boulding, *In Defense of Monopoly* (1945) 59 Q. J. Econ. 524, Comments (1946) 60 Q. J. Econ. 612, 615, 619; Rostow, *supra* note 61, at 587–594.

88. In the second volume of his study, Professor Bain concludes that "the existing degree of competition seems to lead, when unchecked, to an undesirable degree of market instability, and, when privately checked, to somewhat arbitrary and undependable price results," p. 359. No criteria are suggested for determining what degree of price competition is socially desirable, dependable and unarbitrary.

ance of customary prices. Investments have been lavishly and speculatively made in the oil industry, and for high stakes. Great fortunes have been made, and are still being made, in oil, and many units have earned a compensatory, or better than compensatory return on their capital. Should the state interfere to make certain that all such investments are profitable? Specifically, should it interfere to prevent or offset the impact on values of new discoveries or advances in technology, on the one hand, and of price competition on the other?

Obviously, an oil property with a given reserve is worth more before the discovery of a great new pool than afterwards. Its actual value has been changed by the change in the total supply position of the market. Pennsylvania oil properties were worth less after oil was discovered in Oklahoma, just as New England farm land declined in value when the agricultural West was opened up. Such changes can be expected to take place periodically in the oil industry, though perhaps not in the same degree as before. The scale of petroleum output has increased to such an extent that a new pool would have a smaller relative impact on the whole market than in 1926 or 1931. A new East Texas field would constitute a smaller fraction of supply now than at the time of its discovery. Similarly, innovations in drilling technique, by enlarging total ultimate recoveries, alter the value of each existing property. It is hard to see any reason why the state should wish to prevent such changes in value, by keeping production down, and prices up, even if long-term falls in the level of prices should result in the occasional disappointment of some investors in oil stocks or oil properties. In an economy which allows profits, what justification can there be for preventing specific losses of this kind, attributable to risk? Such changes in value are the consequence of new discoveries or of new techniques, i.e., of economic progress. Unless they are allowed to have an effect on prices, society is being denied the advantage of them as effectively as by the suppression of a patent.[89]

There is a second string in Professor Bain's bow: that in the

89. Professor Bain does, however, promise in his third volume (not yet pub-

oil industry not only the irregularity of new discoveries but the pressure of competition itself as a factor determining output would have an unsettling and "destructive" effect on the market. Again it is difficult to see any element in the oil industry, apart perhaps from the rule of capture, which would justify supplanting competition as a primary market force determining the level of production. With the rule of capture replaced by unitization, one would be hard put to devise an economic case for production control as such. There would be no reason for producing units to carry production to uncompensatory levels, for prices to fall to chronically unprofitable levels, or for sellers to undertake a suicidal destruction of capital values. Under a regime of competition, prices would undoubtedly be more flexible than under present controls, at least in a downward direction, in response to great declines in national income. During upturns of the trade cycle they should be less capable of outstripping the rate of increase of income, and thus imposing a check on the course of recovery; although recent experience suggests that monopolistically controlled prices, restrained by fear of anti-trust prosecution, may rise less than free prices under pressure of large scale inflation of money incomes. However, there is no reason to suppose that the existence at any time of large amounts of unused capacity should constitute a justification for permitting sellers to combine to determine the appropriate level of supply. Unutilized production—or "surplus" capacity, in Professor Bain's sense —is necessarily characteristic of most industry. It has not prevented steep price rises in the past, nor steep drops in production, seasonal and otherwise. There is no reason to suppose that it would do so in the future.

The policy of prorationing allowable production on a flat per well basis has a purpose, however, even though it is not a conservation purpose. Dividing the quotas in this way has the effect of restricting the production of the better wells, largely owned by the large companies, in favor of the smaller wells,

lished) to consider the different question of what should be done about the scarcity rents imposed upon the industry by curtailment policy. *Id.*, 358–359.

often owned by independent and non-integrated producers. These are the producers who must sell their product to a refiner, most often a major company. They sell in a market characterized by many independent sellers, and very few buyers, most of whom are large companies entirely aware of their stake in parallel action. The sales of crude oil take place principally in the oil fields, at the end of the pipe line or gathering pipe line, and not in a refinery area or other center where more buyers would be likely to bid. In any given field there may be one, two or a few major companies owning pipe lines, ready to buy crude. Their posted purchase prices show the same pattern of price leadership, subject to varying private deviations at different times, which characterizes the retail market for gasoline, and for the same reasons.[90]

By somewhat restricting the major companies' capacity to produce for themselves, the prorationing authorities correspondingly strengthen the hand of the scattered, independent sellers of crude. They are seeking to redress the balance of power in the market, in favor of the numerous and politically vocal sellers of crude oil. The device is simple and not very effective, for the basic forces determining bargaining positions in the crude market are beyond the reach of state oil control authorities. But the thrust is there, working against many other pressures of the industry.[91]

90. TNEC HEARINGS, Part 14, 7279–7285, 7364–7376, 7417–7423; Part 17, 9766–9770, 9772–9783, 9809–9812, 9943–9944; WATKINS, 124 ff.; O'MAHONEY HEARINGS, *The Independent Petroleum Company* (1946) 78. The comment of an independent refiner on the posted price system says all that really needs to be said about it: "In most fields there is usually one predominant buyer and he sets the price. We naturally are subject to go along with it." TNEC HEARINGS, Part 14, 7352. See Comment (1942) 51 YALE L. J. 608, 621.

Mr. Farish, then President of the Standard Oil Co. (New Jersey), remarked "Oil companies have perhaps refrained too much from the use of price as a means of adjusting supply and demand. . . . No one in the oil industry States wants to initiate a price cut; literally I mean no individual wants to be responsible for initiating a price cut. It is a very unpopular thing to do, and it brings about all kinds of reactions, most of them unpleasant, so there is a tendency to delay the interpretation of a market condition, and the delay makes it worse and, finally, when it does come, why, it is a little bigger than it would have been if it had been taken promptly when the market pressures first began to exert themselves." TNEC HEARINGS, Part 17, 9809–9810.

91. POGUE, ECONOMICS OF THE PETROLEUM INDUSTRY (1939) 27–28, and see *supra*, p. 10 and note 24.

PART III

CONTROLLING THE
PRODUCT MARKETS

THE problem of the major companies is a dual one: to master both the markets in which they buy and the markets in which they sell. They have a stake in keeping to a minimum the effective number of buyers of crude, and sellers of gasoline. Since all crude oil must proceed to the markets via pipe lines or other means of transportation, and through refineries, bulk stations and other media of distribution, the bridgeheads of control are very obvious. And so far it has been entirely possible for the major companies to seize and keep the positions essential to their purpose.

CHAPTER 7

Pipe Lines and Other Means of Transportation

THE major companies have two chief interests in the price of crude. They are generally in favor of production controls, and an adequately high market price, which are the necessary conditions of high retail prices. Under conditions of high production and intense competition in the crude market, it is more difficult for the majors to buy up independently produced crude, which might otherwise be sold to independent refiners and reach the retail market through independent distributors. The major companies know that in the past a relatively small flow of cheap crude through independent refiners to the retail markets has been able to exert a disproportionate influence in the fragile and monopolistic "led" market for gasoline. They realize also that even though they now control a larger share of known reserves than ever before, new fields outside their own areas of control may be discovered, to impose new strains on the price system unless the policy of over-all limitation of production is firmly enforced. In this way they can be reasonably sure that their investments will be protected against great changes in values which might otherwise follow new discoveries of oil, or improvements in extraction technique. On the other hand, the major companies are the purchasers of crude oil, and as such are interested, within the framework of control, in buying as cheaply as they can.

The chief weapon of the major companies for protecting their position in the market for crude oil is their ownership of pipe lines, the indispensable link (except for shore and offshore wells) between the oil well and the refinery. To a lesser but still vital extent, ownership of tankers serves the same purpose of forcing the independent to sell his crude in the field, or to be dependent on independent refiners, weaker and far less effective purchasers of his product. Control of transportation facilities enables the majors to locate their refineries in the market areas, and has remitted non-integrated refineries largely to shifting and unsatisfactory locations in the field. In the late thirties, the major companies owned between 85 and 89 per cent of the important crude oil trunk pipe lines.

The struggle over pipe-line policy has been going on for several generations. Control of transportation facilities was John D. Rockefeller's key weapon, and the strategic importance of transportation has not declined in the oil industry.

The first step in the struggle was thought to be the declaration that pipe lines were common carriers, and therefore required to carry all the oil offered them. This was accomplished after an extended battle in the Hepburn Act of 1906, and later upheld in full dress test litigation by the Supreme Court.[92] Despite strenuous and repeated efforts, however, the Congress has never extended the principle of the Commodities Clause of the Hepburn Act beyond railroads, so that the independent forces in the industry, confronting major company control of the pipe lines, were left to their dubious remedies under the Interstate Commerce Act.

The inadequacy of those remedies to meet the basic problems of monopolistic control in the oil industry is made very plain in two important recent proceedings, the Interstate Commerce Commission's pipe-line investigation,[93] and the consent

92. 34 STAT. 584 (1906), 41 STAT. 474 (1920), 49 U. S. C. § 1 (1940); The Pipe Line Cases, 234 U. S. 548 (1914); Champlin Ref. Co. v. United States, 67 Sup. Ct. 1 (U. S. 1946). See United States House of Representatives, Hearings before Committee on Interstate and Foreign Commerce on H. R. 9676 and H. R. 8572, *Oil and Oil Pipe Lines,* 73d Cong., 2d Sess. (1934); W. BEARD, REGULATION OF PIPE LINES AS COMMON CARRIERS (1941); R. MILLS, PIPE LINES' PLACE IN THE OIL INDUSTRY (1935); Black, *Oil Pipe Line Divorcement by Litigation and Legislation* (1940) 25 CORN. L. Q. 510; Prewitt, *The Operation and Regulation of Crude Oil and Gasoline Pipe Lines* (1942) 56 Q. J. ECON. 177; Whitesel, *Recent Federal Regulation of the Petroleum Pipe Line as a Common Carrier* (1947) 32 CORN. L. Q. 337; Comment (1942) 51 YALE L. J. 1338.

93. Reduced Pipe Line Rates and Gathering Charges, 243 I.C.C. 115 (1940); Minnelusa Oil Corp. v. Continental Pipe Line Company, 258 I.C.C. 41 (1944). See also Petroleum Rail Shippers' Association v. Alton & Southern R. R., 243 I.C.C. 589 (1941).

decree in the *Atlantic Refining Company* case based on the anti-rebate provisions of the Elkins Act.[94]

After a generation or more of prodding, the Interstate Commerce Commission began its investigation of the petroleum pipe-line situation in 1934, and presented its first report in 1940. That report was not a final order requiring action, since the case was later reopened for further hearings, and was pending when last reported in 1944. In itself this chronology is a sufficient comment on the adequacy of the regulatory process to deal with the variable and shifting problems of a dynamic industry.

The case concerned a proposed reduction in the rates and minimum tender requirements of 37 carriers by pipe line, owning 80,000 of the 95,000 miles of interstate pipe lines, as the situation then stood, largely from the Texas and Mid-Continent fields to the North, East and Middle-Western market areas. Of the pipe lines covered by the investigation, 36,000 miles were gathering lines, and 44,000 miles were trunk lines. In all except a few minor instances, the pipe lines were essentially plant facilities of major integrated companies, carrying only, or almost only, oil produced or purchased by affiliates.

The Commission studied costs and earnings, dividends and capitalization. It had elaborate valuations made in cabalistic proceedings based on "due" consideration for original costs, costs of reproduction new, original cost less depreciation, costs of reproduction less depreciation, present value of land and rights and other so-called "elements" of value. The results of these calculations were compared with book values and earnings. In 1935 the carriers were averaging better than 14 per cent a year on what the Commission regarded as "the" value of their properties, although the earnings record was meaningless, since the charges represented by the income accounts were against the carrier itself. Increased tax pressure in the late

94. United States v. Atlantic Refining Co. (1941) 10 U. S. L. WEEK 2403 (D. Col. 1941), Comments (1942) 51 YALE L. J. 1338, 1349; 9 U. OF CHI. L. REV. 503.

thirties brought about a reduction in nominal rates, and a considerable tendency to merge pipe-line affiliate corporations into the major companies themselves.

The Commission proposed two chief remedies: (1) a reduction of minimum tender requirements to levels not to exceed 10,000 barrels, in order to give smaller producers a theoretical chance to use the pipe-line facilities, and thus try to sell their product in larger markets; and (2) a selective reduction of rates to give each pipe-line company a return of about 8 per cent on its approved valuation. The lines were regarded as not competing with each other, and it was felt that no harm would be done by having the rates of each line differ, so long as the level of profit was held down to 8 per cent or thereabouts on each pipe line's approved value. Thus a fantastic rate structure was envisioned, in which the same service would be charged at different rates in different areas, depending largely upon the historical accident of what the various pipe lines happened to cost when they were built. Once more in the process of utility regulation, the rate was based upon a guess as to investment value, not the value on the rate.

That this mouse is the result of all the mountainous efforts over the last twenty-five years to dislodge the rule of *Smyth v. Ames* is confirmed in the *Hope Natural Gas* case, and other recent rate cases in the Supreme Court.[95] The *Hope* case dealt with the efforts of the Federal Power Commission under the Natural Gas Act to reduce the rates for the carriage and in part the sale of natural gas, in this instance gas from West Virginia destined for use in the cities and towns of Pennsylvania and Ohio. Pennsylvania and Ohio were strongly supporting the rate reductions ordered by the Commission, West Virginia as strongly opposed. The Supreme Court upheld orders requiring rate reductions which it was thought would reduce earnings to between 6½ and 8 per cent of the approved rate base.

95. Federal Power Commission v. Hope Natural Gas Co., 320 U. S. 591 (1944). See Hale, *Utility Regulation in the Light of the Hope Natural Gas Case* (1944) 44 COL. L. REV. 488; *id., Commissions, Rates and Policies* (1940) 53 HARV. L. REV. 1103; *id., Does the Ghost of Smyth v. Ames Still Walk?* (1942) 55 HARV. L. REV. 1116.

The company involved in the case was a subsidiary of the Standard Oil Company (New Jersey), which had started with an investment of $17 million, its capital at the time of the litigation consisting of $28 million in par value of common stocks, of which $11 million in par value represented stock dividends. It had an earned surplus of $8 million, had paid nearly $100 million in dividends over 40 years, averaging 20 per cent a year on the original investment, and 12 per cent a year on "average invested capital," plus $46 million in depletion and depreciation charges. In the year previous to the litigation its income was calculated at $5.8 million. The rate base approved by the Court was set at $33.7 million, after a good deal of controversy over items excluded by the Commission as capital, notably an item of $17 millions for drilling wells and other costs originally charged off, and met, as operating expenses.

The court started bravely by denouncing the fallacy of *Smyth v. Ames:* One could hardly set utility rates in order to achieve a fair return on a fair value of the utility properties, since the value of a going enterprise depends on earnings under whatever rates were to be set.[96] Fair value is the end product of the process of rate making, the court remarked, not the starting point. For regulatory purposes, value means only the capitalization of what the utility will be allowed to earn. The issue for the courts in such cases is a limited one, Mr. Justice Douglas said. If the total effect of the rates set could not be said to be unjust and unreasonable, judicial inquiry was at an end. The Court indicated that it wasn't much interested in the rate-making theory the Commission used, although in this case the issue was not confiscation as such, under the due process clause, but conformity with the requirements of a statute. It was held that the rates set were unassailable, because they permitted the company to operate successfully, to maintain its financial integrity, attract capital and compensate its investors for their risks.[97]

Reducing rates in order to reduce profits to a fair return on

96. 320 U. S. at 601.
97. 320 U. S. at 603–605.

a fair value is another lap on the merry-go-round of *Smyth v. Ames*. The volume of business for natural gas pipe lines (and for oil pipe lines to a lesser extent) is sensitive to changes in rates, and for both types of carriers the volume carried varies greatly with the stage of the trade cycle. In the *Hope* case gross revenues had varied from year to year by as much as 30 per cent under fixed rates, and a much larger fluctuation in profits will continue inevitably, since so large a part of pipe line, and other utility, costs are fixed. For oil pipe lines, Interstate Commerce Commission data indicate that nearly 50 per cent of charges are depreciation allowances and other fixed items.[98] Thus under the rule of the *Hope Natural Gas* case, one can expect a constant readjustment of rates to follow the will-o'-the-wisp of fair returns.

The *Hope* case confirms the probable legality of the Interstate Commerce Commission's opinion in its pipe-line investigation. And it underscores the futility of that procedure as a device to reduce monopolistic influence in the oil business. However ruthlessly the *Hope* case will permit regulatory bodies to reduce rates, the rate control approach can make no substantial contribution to the problem of enlarging the area of competition in the petroleum industry. For the basic fact is that today as in the time of the original *Pipe Line* cases in 1914, the pipe lines in the petroleum industry do not exist to make money by transporting oil. They exist to transport oil already owned by the carrier major company, and their rate structure is designed to persuade the independent producer of oil to sell his product in the oil fields, at prices dominated by the major company, or the few major companies owning the pipe line or lines in that field. The pipe-line rates are such as to discourage the seller from paying the costs of carriage on his oil in order to reach a wider market in the refinery area. As Mr. Justice Holmes said in 1914, the Standard Oil Company (in that case) through its control of the pipe lines "made itself master of the

98. 243 I.C.C. at 129-130. For 1938 fixed expenses for the Humble Pipe Line Co. totalled 49.34 per cent of all expenses, and for a group of three Texas pipe line companies 52.53 per cent (depreciation charges, taxes other than income, and fixed and general overhead expenses).

fields without the necessity of owning them and carried across half the continent a great subject of international commerce coming from many owners but, by the duress of which the Standard Oil Company was master, carrying it all as its own." [99]

Even if rates could be forced down low enough to make access to refinery markets possible for independent sellers, and if the state prorationing authorities held down major production, the independents would confront the difficulties of service which were conspicuous in the anthracite fields before the *Reading* cases: the carrier would prefer his own shipments to those of a competitor. The transportation service would be uncertain, and, however low the level of rates, the shipper would be forced to pay his competitor a profit on the carriage. At any level of profits likely to be sanctioned by the Interstate Commerce Commission, such payments would constitute a rebate affecting competition between the oil companies.[100]

Under the best conceivable rate reductions that could be imagined, reduction of pipe-line rates would be a step of limited promise. For even if the independent seller reached across all the hurdles to a somewhat larger market, he would find his position had not been radically improved. He would confront a larger group of possible buyers of his product, but it would still be a small group of buyers, compared with the greatly increased number of sellers who would simultaneously have come with him from the separate oil fields to the common market place. The difference, however, though not revolutionary, might well prove significant. If the independent producers of crude could use the pipe lines on equal terms as shippers, they could more easily do business with independent refiners. The dominance of the major companies as buyers in the crude markets would perhaps be qualified. Thus the monopoly control factors which have steadily cut the independent re-

---

99. 234 U. S. at 559. Compare the similar policy pursued by the anthracite railroads, of buying the coal of potential competitors in the field, and reselling themselves in the market. United States v. Reading Co., 253 U. S. 26, 49–50 (1920).

100. See United States v. Reading Co., note 99 *supra*.

finers' share of the market for the last twenty years would be
partly ameliorated, and the independent refiners would have
gained a less restricted opportunity to compete with the major
refiners. They would have greater access to sources of supply,
and would therefore be less completely under major company
control.[101]

The recent attack on so-called pipe-line profits as an unfair
competitive advantage and a rebate suffers from the same inadequacy of fundamental analysis as the attack on pipe-line
rates. The proceeding was based on the theory that pipe-line
profits, or rather dividends, constituted a rebate to a shipper
prohibited by the Interstate Commerce Act. The government
sued for triple the amount of the alleged rebates, and an injunction against the alleged violations of the statute. The case
was settled by a consent decree in 1941, in which the companies agreed that not more than 7 per cent of the Interstate
Commerce Commission's valuation of the pipe-line properties
is to be paid as dividends in any one year. Any earnings above
that figure are to be segregated and used for working capital,
or for the retirement of debt capitalizing fixed equipment, or
for the construction or purchase of fixed capital equipment,
except that no new facilities thus financed out of profits are to
enter the rate base. The hope of those who drafted the decree

101. Petroleum Rail Shippers' Assoc. v. Alton & Southern R. R., 243 I.C.C.
589 (1941), presents perhaps the most graphic available account of the dynamics
of the struggle between major and independent companies for access to markets, and of the extreme importance of transportation policy to that contest.
That case was a proceeding brought by independent Mid-Continent refiners,
backed by their independent jobber customers, to obtain reductions in the rail
tank-car rates on gasoline between Mid-Continent refining points and Mid-
Western consuming areas. The pipe-line rate structure, previously based on rail
rates, had been gradually reduced during the thirties and, more important, the
actual costs to the major companies of operating their lines had fallen far below
the level of rail rates. Moreover, the appearance of Illinois as a producing area
had weakened the basing-point system of price quotation, resting on the Tulsa
price plus freight from that shipping point. The Commission found that the development and improvement during the thirties of gasoline pipe-line transportation, plus the emergence of Illinois as a producing area, had reduced the "value"
of transportation service via tank car. The independent refiners and jobbers, dependent upon rail transportation, and adapted to it, were threatened with loss
of their competitive position unless rail rates were substantially reduced. They
obtained extensive relief, as to both rail- and pipe-line rates.

evidently was that it would force a rate reduction, although why such hopes were entertained is not at all clear.

The view that under the present organization of the oil industry the whole of pipe-line profits subsidize other parts of the major companies' operations will not bear inquiry.[102] The fact is that to the extent that the pipe-line companies carry petroleum products which they own, pipe-line profits are incurred as a bookkeeping charge without real significance as profits. They are paid by one part of the major oil company to another; the shipper and carrier are the same, the receipts of the carrier being the shipper's nominal costs. They are a component of the major company's ultimate profit only to the extent that receipts upon final sales of the company's products validate the prices charged for crude oil and its transportation.

The level of pipe-lines rates is, however, part of the process of market control, and is one of the weapons which permit the major companies to keep ultimate sale prices at a point which vindicates their nominal pipe-line charges. The level of pipe-line rates is a measure of the forces required to keep posted prices for crude at an appropriate minimum, and above all to keep independent refiners, who must depend on independent sources of crude, on relatively short and expensive rations of supplies. The majors have many times seen how precarious their market controls can be, and how vulnerable to the impact of relatively small amounts of additional supply—as indeed are most monopolistically controlled markets.[103] The vulnerability of such price structures is not a comment on the elasticity of consumer demand for the product, but on the price-making mechanism which has evolved. Given the prevailing pattern of oligopoly, price cuts must be met to avoid adverse shifts in each large seller's share of the market. The major companies

102. The view, however, is generally shared. See Prewitt, *supra* note 92, 199–201; COOK, 21–23, 28.

103. See, e.g., W. Y. ELLIOTT and others, INTERNATIONAL CONTROL IN THE NON-FERROUS METALS (1937); K. KNORR, RAW-MATERIAL PROBLEMS AND POLICIES (1946); *id.*, TIN UNDER CONTROL (1945); *id.*, WORLD RUBBER AND ITS REGULATION (1945); J. W. F. ROWE, MARKETS AND MEN (1936); OUALID, INTERNATIONAL RAW MATERIALS CARTELS: CAUSES, EFFECTS, REGULATION (1938); Eastham, *Rationalization in the Tin Industry* (1936) 4 REV. ECON. STUDIES 13.

own the pipe lines not only as a productive piece of capital equipment, but as a necessary element for the preservation of the special conditions of market structure in the petroleum industry on which price leadership and price maintenance ultimately rest. One can gauge the significance of these controls from a typical experience. In the East Texas field in 1935 there were 74 independent refineries. By 1941 there were only 3, although at least 25 of the original refineries were strong modern plants, technically equipped to stay in the market.[104] In the market for crude oil, the majors are monopsonistic or oligopsonistic buyers; in the markets for refined products they are oligopolists. In both phases of the process they are concerned to limit the potential scope of independent refiners in an industry where entry would be relatively easy, in the absence of such economic pressures.

104. COOK, 33; TNEC HEARINGS, Part 15, 8538.

CHAPTER 8

The Maintenance of Major Company Domination of Refining

THE organization of the refining phase of the industry is another of the crucial elements of market control. The major companies have a prodigious advantage in refining, controlling over 80 per cent of refinery facilities, however the fraction is measured. Their refineries are bigger, in general more modern, and above all better located. Because of the major companies' control of transportation facilities, and what that implies, their refineries can be located in or near consuming markets—permanently economic locations—whereas the independent refiners are most often compelled to locate in the fields near a source of supply, and are thus at a double disadvantage. Their source of supply may shift, imposing a capital loss on them. And they must depend on their competitors for the transportation of their product to the market, unless they use the more expensive transportation facilities, like tank cars or trucks.[105]

It is difficult to measure how much of the advantage of the major companies in refining is due the inherent technological advantage of bigness, and how much to the market advantage of their monopolistic position. Certainly the major companies have accumulated important resources of money, experience and research talent, which help to make their production units more effective. Moreover, they have a commanding advantage in access to and control over both patented information and technological know-how. On the other hand, the care with which the major companies safeguard the bulwarks of their monopoly position suggests that factors of market structure

105. See note 101 *supra*. On the location of independent refineries, see O'MA-HONEY HEARINGS, *The Independent Petroleum Company* (1946) 77, 197–198.

and organization have a good deal to do with maintaining their advantage in refining.

Refining crude oil is done in widely different plants, many of them being relatively small. The basic processes are uniform, or fairly uniform.[106] They involve the distillation, cracking and condensation of crude oil, which in itself has varying physical and chemical properties, into its separate products. The products of the distillation of crude petroleum are in every sense joint products, and the proportion of each can be varied easily depending on the basic properties of the crude oil used, and the adjustment of the refining process. Several processes are in use and in development, especially for cracking and condensation. From the economic point of view the significant fact about these processes is that they are patented or otherwise developed by special technical groups. They are neither technically unique nor especially difficult to use. There is no inherent reason why they cannot be made available to all possible users, and many are so available. It is equally practical for large and for quite small corporations to employ such techniques, if on the same royalty terms. For some purposes, in fact, research and technical skills may be more cheaply available to small companies, through the fees of independent and specialized engineering firms, than to the large companies which maintain their own staffs. Nor are the capital requirements of a good refining plant extraordinarily high. Plants of varying types can be built for between $2 million and $16 to $20 million dollars, not a prohibitive cost requiring the establishment of corporations with several hundred millions of capital. The vital fact is that for different markets and products different types of plants are altogether economic. A refinery capable of making aviation gasoline is not necessary if one is engaged chiefly in the manufacture of asphalt or heating oil. A practical distillation plant may serve a useful purpose and make money on a technically simple basis. On the other hand, a non-integrated company, if well located, can utilize elaborate

106. A. Dunstan and others, The Science of Petroleum (1938) vol. 2–3, 1465–2174; 1 Bain, ch. 5; TNEC Hearings, Part 15, 8619–8670, particularly at 8634–8640; Surplus Property Administration, Report to the Congress, Aviation-Gasoline Plants and Facilities (Jan. 14, 1946), Part 1.

cracking or distillation equipment as efficiently as a major company.[107]

There is no basis in the technology of refining for concluding that the bigness of the big oil companies is the inevitable price we must pay for using modern methods of manufacture. On the contrary, there is every reason to believe that from the point of view of efficiency in operations—cost per unit—smaller firms would be able to operate on a competitive basis if the control of the majors over access to raw materials on the one hand, and to markets on the other were eliminated. To reach such a goal may require the release of some patents now closely held. The rapid recent development of the law of patents in relation to restraints of trade, however, indicates that any present advantage of a major company based on patent position could be eliminated without great difficulty in the context of the monopolistic structure of the petroleum industry.[108] An expansion of independent refining would inevitably stimulate the further development of petroleum engineering firms, providing technical and research services on a fee basis. Engineering consultants have had an extended experience as independent elements in the petroleum industry, and an expansion of their place should serve to free knowledge and technique from some present inhibitions. Such development would be highly desirable, in requiring a market evaluation of a specialized service, and in making advanced technology generally available to all branches of the industry.

107. O'MAHONEY HEARINGS, *The Independent Petroleum Company* (1946) 187–208, 338; TNEC HEARINGS, Part 15, 8539. Methods of refining have been announced "which would enable the smallest refinery in the country to have the latest technological advantage" in catalytic cracking. O'MAHONEY HEARINGS, *Petroleum Requirements—Postwar* (1946) 83.

108. Hartford-Empire Co. v. United States, 323 U. S. 386 (1945); Mercoid Corp. v. Mid-Continent Inv. Co., 320 U. S. 661 (1944); United States v. Masonite Corp., 316 U. S. 265 (1942); Interstate Circuit v. United States, 306 U. S. 208 (1939); Morton Salt Co. v. G. S. Suppiger Co., 314 U. S. 488 (1942); United States v. Univis Lens Co., 316 U. S. 241 (1942). *Cf.* United States v. Bausch & Lomb Optical Co., 321 U. S. 707 (1944). Havighurst, *Legal Status of Industrial Control by Patent* (1941) 35 ILL. L. REV. 495; HAMILTON, PATENTS AND FREE ENTERPRISE, TNEC MONOGRAPH No. 31 (1941); Steffen, *Invalid Patents and Price Control* (1946) 56 YALE L. J. 1; Zlinkoff, *Monopoly Versus Competition* (1944) 53 YALE L. J. 514; Comment (1946) 56 YALE L. J. 77; Notes (1945) 45 COL. L. REV. 422, 601; Comment (1941) 51 YALE L. J. 299. See O. BARNETT, PATENT PROPERTY AND THE ANTI-MONOPOLY LAWS (1943).

CHAPTER 9

Monopolistic Marketing of Gasoline

THE organization of the marketing of petroleum products presents a series of problems in the strategy and tactics of private market control. In view of the dispersal of petroleum marketing units, the size of the market, the steady expansion of demand for petroleum products and the large number of independent firms which enter the industry, the preservation of a consistently monopolistic pattern of pricing and price control on a national basis is an extraordinary achievement.

In this discussion of marketing controls, we shall concentrate on the selling of gasoline, presently the chief petroleum product, and the dominant product in determining market structure.

Gasoline from the refineries is sold through various channels.[109] Much of it—perhaps as much as a quarter in the Mid-Continent Area, a lesser amount in California, and close to a third in the Eastern seaboard market area—is sold to wholesale dealers or jobbers in tank car lots, so called, for transportation to the account of the jobber by pipe line, tanker or tank car in large quantities to the consuming market area. A considerable quantity is sold in smaller lots at bulk storage stations owned by the major company itself, and usually located in or near the consuming market. Such sales are normally made to retail jobbers, or to smaller wholesale jobbers. A good deal is

109. TNEC HEARINGS, Part 14-A, p. 7818; as to California and the Pacific Coast, see 1 BAIN, ch. 6. Bain concludes that the degree of integration and of major company control is such on the West Coast that the "free" domestic tank car market is very small, not more than 10 per cent of total volume. The majors sold 70 per cent of the gasoline consumed in California, the independents about 30 per cent; but 85 per cent of the bulk station distributors, the chief purchasers of gasoline, were linked to their suppliers in various ways. See also 2 BAIN, ch. 8.

More generally, O'MAHONEY HEARINGS, *The Independent Petroleum Company* (1946) 532–536; TNEC HEARINGS, Part 16, 9128–9146, 9347–9367; 8837–8891; 9151–9167; Part 15, 8396–8456, 8671–8718; Part 15-A, *passim*; COLE COMMITTEE HEARINGS, *passim*.

sold directly to large consumers, and distributed by the producing company through retail outlets either owned directly or directly controlled by the major company. An appreciable part of the output of any one major refiner also goes into intercompany exchanges, normally undertaken to save transport costs or to secure stocks for blending, as well as to tide over temporary shortages of the company's own product. According to testimony presented to the TNEC, the average amount of gasoline thus interchanged was about 5 per cent of the total domestic supply. In California the importance of the practice seems to have been even greater.[110]

A series of conventional trade discounts governs the relationship between prices at the several levels of distribution, and much of the litigation and lobbying in the politics of the industry concerns the size of these discounts.[111]

The appearance of these statistics, however, is altogether misleading. The basic measure of retail price control in the industry is the tied outlet. What seems statistically to be distribution through independent jobbing companies is almost always controlled distribution in fact, with the potentialities of price competition between the ultimate distributors severely limited. It is estimated that over 80 per cent of wholesale outlets are in fact tied to a major company.[112] In almost all markets the underlying pattern is the same: the bulk of the product is supplied by a few large sellers; almost all the balance by a large group of intermediate-sized sellers; a small fraction by the noisy fringe of small independents. Some of the intermediate-sized sellers are also subsidiaries of the majors, organized to participate for them in any price wars which may develop, and to share in the market for unbranded products, which usually sell at slight discounts. The conventional pricing procedure in the industry is for a differential to exist in favor of the products advertised and sold by a major company, even though

110. TNEC Hearings, Part 14-A, 7737, 7806–7811; Part 16, 9141–9142, 9145–9146, 9366–9367; Part 17, 9864–9926. For California, see 1 Bain, 131.
111. See, for example, In re Standard Oil Company of Indiana, Federal Trade Commission Docket No. 4389, C. C. H. Trade Regulation Reporter, vol. 3, ¶ 13295, 13447, 13492 (1945–1946).
112. TNEC Hearings, Part 16, 8885; and see note 29 *supra*.

they often come from the same tank as the gasoline sold by the seller of other brands, or of unbranded products.

Jobbers, wholesale or retail, are in all markets almost invariably tied to a single major company source of supply. They are identified through the labelling on their trucks, letter-heads and business premises by the signs and symbols of their supplier. Although normally independent in ownership, they are for every purpose of price policy controlled by their suppliers. Publicly branded as "Tydol" or "Gulf" or "Socony" dealers, they find a switch from one to another of the major companies difficult, and often impossible.

The achievement of this relationship has been a considerable legal feat. Section 3 of the Clayton Act, after all, prohibits any person engaged in commerce, in the course of such commerce, to lease or sell, or contract to sell, any goods, wares, merchandise, machinery, supplies or other commodities, patented or unpatented, or to fix a price, discount or rebate in such sale, on the condition that the lessee or purchaser will not deal in the goods of competitor of the lessor or seller, where the effect of the transaction may be to lessen competition or to create a monopoly in any line of commerce.[113] The statute has presented two major areas of controversy, one to define the exclusive selling arrangements prohibited by the act, the other to determine what the word "may" means in the limitation that such arrangements are condemned only when they may restrict competition. The Supreme Court has until recently been most unsympathetic to Section 3 of the Clayton Act, and the cases of twenty years ago have permitted exclusive sales arrangements to become deeply entrenched in the mores of American business, particularly in the oil business.[114] While recent cases

113. 38 STAT. 731 (1914); 15 U. S. C. § 14 (1940).
114. Federal Trade Commission v. Curtis Pub. Co., 260 U. S. 568 (1923); Federal Trade Commission v. Sinclair Ref. Co., 261 U. S. 463 (1923). For cases upholding the application of the Act, see United Shoe Machinery Corp v. United States, 258 U. S. 451 (1922), aff'g, 264 Fed. 138 (E. D. Mo. 1920), 234 Fed. 127 (E. D. Mo. 1916); International Business Machines Corp. v. United States, 298 U. S. 131 (1936); Fashion Originators' Guild of America v. Federal Trade Commission, 312 U. S. 457 (1941). See Mercoid Corp. v. Mid-Continent Inv. Co., 320 U. S. 661 (1944); Mercoid Corp. v. Minneapolis Honeywell Reg. Co., 320 U. S. 680 (1944); Comment (1946) 56 YALE L. J. 77, 110-119.

have somewhat altered the current of decision, defiance of the Clayton Act is well established practice in the oil industry, based partly on the earlier decisions, and partly on force majeure. Most sales of gasoline at wholesale, and especially the sales of major companies, are very definitely tied sales, and it is the conceded policy of the major companies to make them tied sales to as large an extent as possible, both at the wholesale and the retail level.[115]

The legal devices used to accomplish this result are of considerable variety, and are constantly changing. Some have been approved by the Supreme Court, at least by the Supreme Court of the Taft and Hughes era, as outside the reach of the Clayton Act.

Some fall within the category of so-called agency sales, in which the buyer is nominally rewarded by a commission, rather than a profit. The difference is not very substantial in a business where transactions habitually take place on the basis of conventional mark-ups and discounts, and profit is determined in any event more by volume—gallonage—than by changes in price. The Supreme Court early held that an agency arrangement was not a "lease or sale" within the meaning of the Clayton Act.[116] While other cases indicate a willingness on the part of the justices to ignore the agency form where goods are in fact being distributed commercially in the familiar pattern of wholesale dealings,[117] the hint of these opinions has not yet had its effect on commercial practice. Agencies are used a good deal in the oil business, for direct distribution. But the market is too big, and the appeal of independent action too strong, for agency to be an adequate device of control.

The tying device is often attached explicitly to a contract of sale. Long-term supply contracts are increasingly employed, often as the equivalent of requirement contracts, that is, agree-

---

115. TNEC HEARINGS, Part 17, 9723, 9737-42, 9744-9748; Part 15, 8401-8404; Black, *Exclusive Dealer Devices in the Marketing of Petroleum Products* (1940) 29 GEO. L. J. 439.

116. Federal Trade Commission v. Curtis Pub. Co., 260 U. S. 568 (1923). See also United States v. General Electric Co., 272 U. S. 476 (1926).

117. Standard Fashion Co. v. Magrane Houston Co., 258 U. S. 346 (1922); United States v. Masonite Corp., 316 U. S. 265 (1942).

ments that the buyer will buy all the oil he may need from the seller. While the Supreme Court has declared substantially like provisions to be illegal under the Clayton Act,[118] as comparable in every way to agreements not to buy the goods of a competitor of the seller, there has been no sustained attack on practices like these in the oil industry, perhaps because other ways to tie the jobber to the major company are quite freely available.

In considerable part, the tying arrangements in the oil industry are conventional rather than contractual. The buyer receives pumps, paint, brand signs and other tattoos which identify him in the market as the distributor of a particular major company. The Supreme Court considered the legality of such tying techniques twenty-four years ago, and upheld them, in a supremely unrealistic opinion by Justice McReynolds.[119] That case has since been qualified, but not overruled, and remains one of the fixed points determining the organization of the oil industry.[120] The *Sinclair* case concerned the practice of leasing tanks and pumps to retail dealers on condition that they would use the equipment only with gasoline supplied by the lessor. This, the Court said, did not oblige the operator of the filling station not to deal in the gasoline of a competitor of the major. He was always free to buy or lease another pump, which was not expensive, and from such a pump he could dispense gasoline supplied by someone else. The Court's point ignores the reality. It is not the cost of the second pump which is vital, but the fact that once a dealer is tied and branded, a shift in suppliers is a major step of policy. It is often difficult, expensive and controversial to accomplish.[121]

In a good many cases the tying arrangement is built on or

118. International Business Machines Corp. v. United States, 298 U. S. 131, 135 (1936).

119. Federal Trade Commission v. Sinclair Ref. Co., 261 U. S. 463 (1923).

120. International Business Machines Corp. v. United States, 298 U. S. 131, 135 (1936).

121. Cole Committee Hearings, 35–45, 119–132; TNEC Hearings, Part 16, 9171–9195.

bulwarked by a financial interest in the jobbing company on the part of the supplier. There may be an extension of credit, or a note, or a stock purchase which gives the supplier a voice in the affairs of the purchaser.[122] Quite commonly such acquisitions of a financial interest are made to curb exuberant price cutting policies indulged in by an independent wholesaler, who becomes subdued after his dependence on his supplier is made more explicit.

The tying arrangements in the field of wholesaling have their counterparts at the retail level, both as to jobbers and service station outlets. Here the legal forms take on more variety and ingenuity, not alone because of the Clayton Act, but for other legal reasons: to avoid coverage under the National Labor Relations Act, the Fair Labor Standards Act, or the Social Security Act; to minimize income taxation or to escape chain store taxes. It is now common to have the filling station nominally owned by its operator, but controlled in fact by the major company supplying gasoline, through complicated double leases, or other elaborate procedures for avoiding the obvious.[123]

The net result is the organization of a vast market around the polarizing position of the major companies—5 to 16 in each consuming market, the modal number being 11 [124]—selling a uniform and standardized product through tied outlets of various kinds, except for a small, carefully watched flow of gasoline sold as private brands, and in part produced by independent refiners. Large forces of potentially independent and competitive units in the industry are thus mobilized into regiments wearing the uniform of one or another of the major companies. So equipped, they march in step, following the price policy of the major companies. The competitive potential of the market is transformed. Every member shares to a lesser or greater degree the profits of a monopolistic price policy. In fact, the market consists not of many separate dealers

---

122. See, e.g., Atlantic Ref. Co. v. Hodgman, 13 F. (2d) 781 (C.C.A. 3d, 1926).
123. TNEC Hearings, Part 16, 9357–9360.
124. Cook, 41, 88–89, 91–94.

and jobbers, but of the few major company phalanxes, combining large numbers of scattered sellers into effectively disciplined units.

The pricing practices which prevail in such a market of a few sellers are naturally those of price leadership and limited competition. In most areas the prevailing price is at or near the price posted by one or another of the big sellers. The fact implicit in the structure of the market, that any price cut can and will be met by other large sellers, is a sufficient force to deter frequent or aggressive price competition. Under the circumstances, price competition seems to promise no major seller additional profit, since all sellers tend to underestimate the elasticity of demand for their product. The independents do not protest at monopolistic control as such, but only at pressure on their discounts, which reduces their share of monopoly profit. The major sellers attempt to change their share of the market largely through advertising, multiplication of selling outlets, and the development of consumers' preferences. Selling costs of this type are incurred as an alternative to price competition. In the oil industry they have developed to grotesque extremes, both as advertising expenditures, and in the building of offset filling stations at every conceivable corner where traffic might pass in sufficient volume. The manifest wastes of such behavior raise the question whether in many cases monopolistic competition may not be more costly to society than monopoly itself.

Two recent anti-trust cases permit one to observe the dynamic functioning of the gasoline market in vivid detail. They illustrate both the promise and the shortcomings of the anti-trust remedy in the oil industry, for they are instances in which the purpose of the litigation was frustrated by the inadequacy of the economic conception on which the cases depended.

The first of these cases is *United States v. Socony-Vacuum Oil Company*.[125] The *Socony-Vacuum* case was one of a pair

125. 310 U. S. 150 (1940), *reversing* 105 F. (2d) 809 (C.C.A. 7th, 1939). Notes (1940) 49 YALE L. J. 761; (1941) 89 U. OF PA. L. REV. 683; (1940) 34 ILL. L. REV. 619; (1942) 51 YALE L. J. 1338.

The author should point out that he was associated with counsel for some of the defendants in this case for several months in 1937 and 1938.

of related criminal proceedings concerned with major company price policy in the entire Mid-Continent market for petroleum products—an area of 10 states, including Illinois, Michigan, Minnesota, Wisconsin, and other important centers of population and business. The supplies of this consuming area were derived largely from the north-central oil fields of Oklahoma, Kansas and Northern Texas. Since the products of the more southerly fields, which normally moved to the Gulf ports, would flow north if the price relation between the two markets varied by ⅛ of a cent a gallon, the control plan under attack in the *Socony-Vacuum* case extended to the East Texas field as well as to the ones directly engaged in supplying the Mid-Continent markets.

The case concerns an important period in the evolution of our present market controls. It deals with part of the total effort represented by the N.R.A. experiment in the oil industry to establish effective restrictions on the output of crude petroleum, and directs attention to the central importance of higher prices and price control as the true purpose of the program of controlling output. Beginning in 1933, the N.R.A. authorities put together in working form a plan for "restoring prosperity" to the oil industry. They utilized the policies, ideas and experiments which some elements in government and in the industry had been urging for a decade. The basic control technique was limitation of output to estimates of "market demand." Such limitations were enforced by the oil producing states, working together, and backed by a federal prohibition against the interstate shipment of "hot" oil, produced in violation of state restriction orders. The N.R.A. authorities soon discovered that there were powerful incentives for oil producers to extract oil in excess of their quotas, and for independent refiners, largely using such cheap oil, to sell gasoline below desired market prices. These transactions were altogether economic and profitable to the individuals concerned, but they were intensely irritating to control authorities anxious to raise prices to preconceived notions of "parity" or "just" levels. As part of the effort to enforce the limitation on output, and keep the "disturbing" influence of cheaper gasoline off the market, the idea of a concerted buying program developed. The large companies would purchase a little more gasoline from independent refiners than they would otherwise have purchased, and perhaps refine a little less themselves. The independent refiners, assured of a market at higher prices, would be under less pressure to seek bargains in crude, and thus make the production controls themselves more workable. The idea of such buying programs as "stabilization" devices had been tried successfully in the extraordinary California market, where it has in effect drastically reduced the number of sellers of gasoline, and thus strengthened the price level.[126]

Two such buying programs were organized as part of the N.R.A. effort, one for the East Texas field and the other in the Mid-Continent area. Trade associations of the independent refiners were utilized as the clearing agencies for notifying the major companies of the gasoline which the independent refiners needed to sell to them, or alternatively, to sell to the market at somewhat lower prices. Each major company picked, or was assigned, an independent refiner from whom it would buy as the occasion required. Possibly the most damaging bit of testimony in the case was the remark of one of the major oil men, who said the plan was like a country dance, in which each major company would pick a regular dancing partner from among the wallflowers who found themselves sitting out the dances. The point was put too vividly to be obscured.

The buying programs were continued after the N.R.A. was declared unconstitutional. There was some evidence that certain officials of the Department of the Interior, still interested in price "stabilization," knew about the continuance of these efforts, and perhaps encouraged them. It would hardly have been remarkable, for the Department, which contained the Code Authority for the industry under N.R.A., had developed pronounced institutional attitudes and policies on oil questions over a period of more than ten years—attitudes fa-

126. See note 58 *supra.*

voring industrial self-organization and production controls, and opposing the anti-trust bias of the Department of Justice. These attitudes have since been strengthened by the war experience of the Department, and persist today.

The buying programs appealed to the major companies for many reasons. For one thing, they tended to weaken the ties between the independent refiners and the jobbers. The buying programs inevitably turned the jobbers more towards the major companies for the supplies they had previously obtained from the independent refiners.

The basic and peculiar appeal of the buying programs to the major companies, however, depended on the way in which gasoline was marketed at wholesale in the Mid-Continent area. All—or almost all—the gasoline distributed in this area by the major companies to jobbers, both wholesale and retail, was sold under contracts, the price term of which was governed by the so-called "open market" quotations for gasoline sold in what was called the spot tank car gasoline market, and reported daily in the trade journals. This spot market consisted of the transactions in which independent refiners sold their product, at Tulsa or other field refinery points, largely to independent jobbers. The price leader in the market—the Standard Oil Company of Indiana—based its posted retail price for any day on the spot market price plus transportation and taxes plus 5½ cents. The jobber's margin was 2 cents and the service station margin 3½ cents. Less than 5 per cent of the gasoline consumed in the market areas was sold in such spot market transactions. The major companies, which before the "stabilization" program had purchased about 12 per cent of the gasoline sold in this way, bought about 50 per cent of the product under the program. They called it "distress" gasoline, which otherwise would have been sold competitively. They did not deliberately bid up the prices in these purchases; they did, however, prevent them from falling. The gasoline involved in these transactions was used and resold in the course of their business. The net effect of the program was to fortify the prices at which the gasoline sold by the majors—83 per cent of the total consumed in the area—went to jobbers, distributors, and ultimately the public. Because of the fact that all prices were based on spot market price quotations, the majors found that by buying a few thousand gallons of gasoline without bargaining too hard, they could increase the prices at which they sold many millions of gallons for their own account.

This remarkable form of self-levitation came under attack indirectly by the jobbers. The pressure for the cases was not addressed to the buying programs as such, nor even to major company domination of price policy. It arose out of a nationwide tendency on the part of the major companies to reduce jobber margins during the depression. The major companies as a group incurred losses, at least by the tax measure, during one year of the depression, and their profits were decidedly low during a period of two or three years.[127] They reacted by attempting to increase their margins at the expense of their wholesale and retail jobbing discounts. In the part of the country concerned in the *Socony-Vacuum* case, there were some 4,000 jobbers through whom about half the gasoline in the market was distributed. Most of the product sold by these jobbers came from the 12 major company defendants in the proceeding. The response of the jobbers to the attack on their margins was vehement and unmistakable. They embarked on a full-scale program of political and economic resistance, utilizing every measure available to a resourceful and enterprising modern lobby. Their congressmen and state legislators heard, and sometimes echoed their demands for the divorcement of marketing from refining, and for anti-chain-store legislation. They complained to the Department of Justice, the newspapers, and to the public at large. The *Socony-Vacuum* case was one phase of their counter-attack—an attack which continued on many fronts until the recovery period after 1938, when rising profits eased the pressure on jobbers' margins. The independent jobbers were not fighting monopolistic control of price policy by the major companies, but the attempt of the majors to take what the jobbers re-

127. COOK, 61.

garded as an undue share of the resulting profit. The independents were not knights crusading in the sacred cause of competition, but beneficiaries of prevailing price practices, seeking to improve their position under the umbrella of privately controlled prices.

There were two indictments in the original *Socony-Vacuum* case.

The first charged a conspiracy to achieve uniform contracts governing the sale of gasoline to jobbers, the level of jobber discounts, and other provisions of their business dealings, to the end of eliminating competition between the major companies in their sale of gasoline to jobbers, and of restricting the ability of jobbers to compete with each other. The indictment charged that the majors agreed on uniform and parallel action regarding the duration of contracts; the provisions for determining the price term of such contracts; the adoption of the procedure of selling f.o.b. Tulsa, regardless of the origin of the gasoline; the size of margins and the relationship between jobber and dealer margins; and a uniform policy for boycotting jobbers who failed to maintain refiner's prices. A plea of *nolo contendere* was entered to this indictment, a fine was paid, and no further proceedings were had.[128]

The second indictment concerned the buying programs. The Supreme Court dealt firmly with the episode, upholding the conviction of most of the defendants. Its opinion restored the damage which the *Appalachian Coals* case had done to the Sherman Act, and reasserted the doctrine of *United States v. Trenton Potteries Company*.[129] While it was perfectly clear, the court said, that only unreasonable restraints of trade were illegal, any restraint which carried with it the power to control prices was inherently unreasonable, without reference to the reasonableness of the prices established, or other circumstances. That these buying programs were part of the "stabilization" efforts of the N.R.A. was deemed immaterial, since

128. United States v. Socony-Vacuum Oil Co., Inc., Indictment No. 11364 (W. D. Wis., 1936).

129. 273 U. S. 392 (1927). Appalachian Coals, Inc. v. United States, 288 U. S. 344 (1933).

they were continued after the sanction of N.R.A. was withdrawn. The approval or knowledge of various officers of the Department of the Interior was held not to favor the defendants, since such officials lacked the power to waive the requirements of the Sherman Act in their efforts to help the oil industry—an argument which met the defendants' case of "reasonableness" obliquely, but nonetheless with decisive force.

The power to control prices which brought the case within the scope of the *Trenton Potteries* policy was a limited one. That the activities of the defendants had a substantial influence on retail prices was enough. They effectively prevented prices from falling, even if they did not accomplish a positive rise in prices. And the defendants had certainly learned a technique, and asserted a power, to control the entire range of retail prices through their leverage over spot market prices. The *Appalachian Coals* case was distinguished on the ground that the defendants in that case had control of a far smaller portion of market supply—in fact, that in the *Appalachian Coals* case the combination was legal *because* it lacked the power to accomplish its major professed purpose, the raising of prices.[130]

From the point of view of policy and analysis, the first question suggested by the case is why the price control device employed by the defendants worked at all. Why did the minute Tulsa spot market for gasoline have so much influence on the price structure of the entire retail market? At first glance, this seems like a case of the tail wagging the dog. The price term of scattered sales involving less than 5 per cent of the gasoline sold was apparently the key to the entire system of price making in the market. Was this an example of the economist's famous principle of marginal analysis, in which the final unit sold in the market is sometimes thought to exercise a decisive influence on price? Not in any simple way, since the economist uses analysis at the margin in this sense as a way of viewing the interplay of forces determining the scale of output, not of price directly. Could the plan have worked without concerted

130. 310 U. S. at 214–216; Appalachian Coals, Inc. v. United States, 288 U. S. 344, 373 (1933). See Rostow, *supra* note 61, at 560–561.

action by the defendants, or does it represent an exploitation on their part of inherent tendencies and potentialities of the petroleum market, in view of its structure, and the balance of power within it?

It seems safe to conclude that the buying programs worked as they did not because the spot market necessarily dominated the retail markets, but because the major companies, through their size and relative fewness of number, were able to dominate both the spot and the retail markets. The plan could not have worked except in a context of monopolistic competition, price leadership and market control by a few dominant sellers. It could not have worked if the spot market embraced a considerably larger share of production.

The flow of oil through independent refiners is an important element in the market structure. A relatively small increase in that flow can touch off price wars which have to be met, even though the resources behind the threat are small. There is always the possibility for the majors to guard against that a larger share of output will be diverted to such channels. The technique of the buying programs involved in the *Socony-Vacuum* case was therefore a way of dealing directly with the problem of the output of independent refiners, by protecting the retail market against downward price pressures originating in that quarter. The prevailing methods of price quotation were only one of a number of alternative ways in which the economic power inherent in the size of the major companies could be asserted. Major company control would have been as complete, and as precarious, if the posted prices of Standard of Indiana were based on the Company's judgment of what the market would bear, rather than on the haphazard spot market quotations. Whatever the nominal structure of the price clause of the contracts between the major companies and their jobbers, the major companies would be forced in their price policy to take some cognizance of the independent sector of the market. To the limit of its capacity, it was a potential alternative source of supplies for jobbers, and the source also of price reducing impulses in the retail market.

If the price structure were favorable, the trend in independent refining could easily be reversed. Entry was cheap, if the independent could achieve access to crude oil, and to the consuming market. The entire system of maintaining tied outlets, and of minimizing the independent area of the market, required a price policy which accurately measured the potential of the independent refiners, and made it more profitable for them to follow the leader than to seek volume by price shading.

Thus the thrust of the case was misconceived. The *Socony-Vacuum* case dealt with a manifestation of economic power, not with its source—with a trade practice, not with the structural organization which permitted the trade practice to work. Its practical consequences were therefore limited, especially because as a criminal proceeding it did not result in a detailed decree capable of review and continuing enforcement.

The second major recent anti-trust litigation in oil was *Ethyl Gasoline Corporation of America v. United States*,[131] a case which contributes a good deal of light on the ways in which the system of price leadership works in the industry. Half the stock of the Ethyl Gasoline Corporation of America was owned by the Standard Oil Company (New Jersey), the rest by General Motors. It held patents on Ethyl fluid, its manufacture, and its combination with gasoline to make higher octane fuel for internal combustion engines. In exploiting its patent, Ethyl chose to manufacture the fluid itself, rather than to license its manufacture by others. The fluid was sold by it to refining companies for combination with gasoline. Sales were made through requirement contracts which bound the purchasing refiners not to sell the combined product except to other licensed refiners, to approved jobbers, approved retail dealers, or to consumers. There were clauses in the sales contracts requiring the purchasers of the Ethyl fluid to comply with certain health practices in using the fluid. The main terms of the contract, however, were economic. They prescribed various conditions on which jobbers would be denied licenses to handle the Ethyl fluid, and thus the Ethyl gasoline,

131. 309 U. S. 436 (1940).

according to the uniform contracts under which Ethyl fluid was sold to refiners. Jobbers would be denied licenses, the Ethyl Corporation prescribed, if they were "unethical" merchants—"unethical," the court found, meaning "willing to engage in price competition." Ethyl gasoline would also be denied to any seller who failed to observe the prevailing two-cent retail price differential in favor of Ethyl gasoline. Moreover, it was provided that if jobbers changed their source of supply by switching from one major supplier to another, they would have to obtain a new license—a requirement which established an additional pressure discouraging any departures from the prevailing system of tied outlets. An elaborate program of inspecting and checking the trade practices of jobbers was set up to enforce the conditions of the contract.

Ethyl fluid was sold by a corporation dominated by the largest major company, and the company with the biggest stake in the system of price leadership and price control. The terms of sale were such as to establish an extra sanction for policing that system of price making. The Ethyl Corporation's defense was that the sales contracts were reasonably adapted to its primary and legitimate purpose of making as much money as possible from its concededly valid patents, and to its equally legitimate purpose of protecting its trade name and reputation, by enforcing health regulations in the use of the Ethyl fluid, and preserving a suitable price differential for the high-test gasoline containing its fluid.

The court upheld an injunction against continued recourse to the restrictive contract terms. The Ethyl Corporation's power to exclude persons from dealing in Ethyl-treated gasoline, Chief Justice Stone said, could not be exercised in the interest of maintaining the price of untreated gasoline, nor the resale price of treated gasoline. The particular way in which the corporation chose to exploit its patent carried certain limiting consequences. Ethyl sold the fluid to refiners. Apparently it could not control the refiners' price policy in subsequent sales. This aspect of the case is puzzling. If one views the transaction as one licensing the refiners to combine Ethyl fluid and gasoline, under Ethyl's combination patent, Ethyl might well have claimed the power to control at least the first sale by the refiners of Ethyl-treated gasoline.[132]

However, the Court held, the actual practice adopted by the Ethyl Corporation in using its patents had decisive consequences. The patent which it chose to exploit was the patent on the fluid, and not on the combination of Ethyl fluid and unleaded gasoline. In utilizing the invention covered by the fluid patent, it could not undertake to control the terms on which refiners, who had bought the patented fluid, sold treated gasoline to jobbers. Most of the opinion is given over to the effect of clauses permitting Ethyl to deny Ethyl-treated gasoline to jobbers who were classed as unethical. This, the Court said, came within the prohibition of the rules which have been developed from the *Carbice* and like cases,[133] in that it represented an attempt on the part of the patentee to use one patent —on the fluid—in order to exploit another—on lead-treated fuel. The special patent power of the patentee was exhausted by the sale of the fluid to refiners, and by the sales of the fuel to the jobbers. Beyond that point, the patents gave no permissible market leverage. What Ethyl was doing here, the Court held, was to employ its patent position as the basis for controlling jobber prices, and suppressing competition among jobbers, in their sales of treated and untreated gasoline. The benefits of the regulation did not accrue to the patentee directly, as a reward for the invention, but to all the major refiners. Thus the restriction was held illegal, as not being addressed primarily to increasing the patent holder's rewards from its invention, but to restraining competition in an area outside the scope of the patent monopoly.

Here again, however, the case apparently made little prac-

132. See Bement v. National Harrow Co., 186 U. S. 70 (1902); United States v. General Electric Co., 272 U. S. 476 (1926); United States v. Masonite Corp., 316 U. S. 265 (1942); Sola Electric Co. v. Jefferson Electric Co., 317 U. S. 173 (1942); MacGregor v. Westinghouse Elec. & Mfg. Co., 67 Sup. Ct. 421 (U. S. 1947); United States v. United States Gypsum Co., 53 F. Supp. 819, 67 *id.* 397 (D. Col. 1943, 1945) *probable jurisdiction noted,* 67 Sup. Ct. 371 (U. S. 1946).

133. Carbice Corp. v. American Patents Development Corp., 283 U. S. 27 (1931).

tical difference to the industry. Ethyl-treated gasoline still sells in most places at a two-cent differential above untreated gasoline, because a sufficient number of consumers are willing to pay that much more for the treated gasoline, despite a much smaller difference in cost to the refiner. Few sellers can fail to observe that they have an interest in exploiting and preserving the public's carefully built-up preference for Ethyl-treated gasoline. Moreover, the major companies still have the power to deny Ethyl gasoline to an offender against the code of the follow-the-leader. The power is now shared by Standard of New Jersey with the other major petroleum companies; but that is hardly a vital distinction in fact, since the major companies are entirely conscious of their equal interest in the status quo, so far as price policy is concerned.

Thus both these famous victories for the government were futile, in that they effected no important change in the price behavior of the industry. They were addressed to symptoms and manifestations of monopoly power, not to its sources. They could accomplish no diminution in the extent or effectiveness of private price control in the industry, and could not even eliminate the price practices to which they were nominally addressed.

CHAPTER 10

The Mother Hubbard Case

APPARENTLY profiting from its experience in the *Ethyl* and other recent oil cases, the Department of Justice in 1940 filed a more radical challenge to the forces of monopoly in the petroleum industry—a general equity proceeding against the American Petroleum Institute and its major company members as a combination reaching towards monopolistic powers in the industry. The case was suspended by the war, and was restored to the docket in 1946.

The complaint is addressed to the American Petroleum Institute, 22 major company defendants, their chief subsidiaries, and the most important individual officers of these organizations. The scope of the complaint is broad. It alleges that the major companies dominate each phase of the industry, by reason of their size, integration, and their use of various restrictive and illegal devices, such as tying clauses, price fixing, and the restriction of production. The statistical and information services of the institute are alleged to be devices for curtailing output even below the level set by state law, and limiting refinery operations. Price leadership is asserted as an offense, both in the crude and in the gasoline markets, and the majors' ownership of pipe lines is attacked on various grounds, including rebates, minimum tenders, and the alleged pressure of the majors to keep rail rates for independents high and for major companies low. Major company domination of wholesale and retail distribution is attacked under the Clayton Act and the Robinson Patman Act, and the process of price formation throughout the industry is described as price fixing. What is under attack is "the present structure of the oil industry"—as a monopoly, as well as a combination in restraint of trade. Apart from its prayer, the complaint makes no reference to the use of the major companies' patents as instruments of monopoly power, nor to the interconnections between American and foreign oil companies. Nonetheless, it presents the most important attempt to use the Sherman Act since the ill-fated case against the United States Steel Corporation.

But the prayer for relief is puzzling, inadequate and disappointing. It was drawn before the recent decisions in the *Aluminum* and *Tobacco* cases, and should be reconsidered in the light of those opinions.

For, having alleged that the companies had monopolistic power by reason of their size, the prayer for relief is limited to requests for injunctions against trade practices, not for a reorganization of the industry in the interest of freeing its competitive potentialities. The attack, once more, is made upon the symptoms and not the sources of power. If all the relief requested were obtained, the decree could have little more effect than the decisions in the *Socony-Vacuum* or *Ethyl* cases. Injunctions against the use of economic power can hardly prevent its assertion in other forms—without combination, and simply in response to the pressure of self-interest.

The proceeding against the defendants named in this complaint was reported suspended in December, 1946, however, apparently in favor of separate actions against specific practices and specific groups of defendants.[134] If such a policy is pursued, the Department of Justice will have largely abandoned the opportunities of procedure and of doctrine presented by the *Tobacco* case, in its most promising chance for their utilization.

134. New York Times, December 18, 1946, p. 32, col. 2. It has been suggested, however, that the purpose of the proposed action is to strengthen and not to weaken the character of the attack under the anti-trust laws. Ralph, *Regional Suits Planned to Replace "Mother Hubbard" Anti-trust Case* (Dec. 28, 1946) 45 OIL AND GAS JOURNAL 140.

CHAPTER 11

Quantitative Measures of Monopoly Power

THUS far we have examined the nature and effect of monopolistic forces in the petroleum industry largely through an analytical description of market behavior, and of market structure as it has evolved historically. The conclusions suggested by that analysis can be checked statistically in several ways, despite the inherent limitations of existing techniques for the quantitative measure of monopoly influences, particularly as applied to the oil industry.

In administering the Sherman Act, the judges have tended to test the presence of monopoly power in part by invoking various rules of thumb: the number of sellers, the extent to which they control market supply directly, and so on. Such a view of the problem is misleading and mechanical. The first economic evil of monopoly—divergence from the allocation of resources and of income which would obtain under perfect competition—may prevail whenever sellers are able to exploit market conditions by controlling price and adjusting output in their own interest. A conclusion as to whether they are achieving monopolistic results depends upon a dynamic evaluation of the market process as a whole, not upon the presence or absence of any particular badge of monopoly power.

Various quantitative or semi-quantitative measures of monopoly have, however, been suggested in recent years.[135] Those which are theoretically most satisfactory are most diffi-

135. G. C. Means, Industrial Prices and Their Relative Inflexibility, Sen. Doc. No. 13, 74th Cong., 1st Sess. (1935); *id., Basic Structural Characteristics and the Problem of Full Employment*, in National Resources Planning Board, The Structure of the American Economy, Part II (1940) 3; A. NEAL, INDUSTRIAL CONCENTRATION AND PRICE INFLEXIBILITY (1942); THORP and others, THE STRUCTURE OF INDUSTRY, TNEC MONOGRAPH No. 27 (1941); Bain, *The Profit Rate as a Measure of Monopoly Power* (1941) 55 Q. J. ECON. 271; Dunlop, *Price Flexibility and the 'Degree of Monopoly'* (1939) 53 Q. J. ECON. 522; Galbraith, *Monopoly Power and Price Rigidities* (1936) 50 Q. J. ECON. 456; Lerner, *The Concept of Monopoly and the Measurement of Monopoly Power* (1934) 1 REV. ECON. STUDIES 157;

cult to use empirically: they cannot be applied, as Professor A. P. Lerner has remarked in another context, "to drown . . . theory in irrelevant statistics." [136] Others, which rest on less satisfactory theoretical foundations, also present fundamental questions of statistical technique. Nonetheless, the attempt to apply the several measures of monopoly power to the oil industry is not altogether without value, at least in a qualitative and impressionistic way.

One approach to the problem of devising statistical measures of monopoly power is to examine price series, and particularly the relative flexibility of prices for different commodities. The differential response of different price series to variations in the level of national income may be of some interest as evidence of monopolistic power over prices, especially if due consideration is given to the conditions of cost and demand for the product, and to the variable impact on different industries of the chief phenomenon of depressions, the decline in the demand for capital goods. However, the usefulness of a good deal of the literature on differential price flexibility has been reduced by its dependence upon dubious assumptions about price behavior. Much of it rests on oversimplified premises to the general effect that in competitive market situations (other things being assumed to remain equal) prices would be flexible in response to changes in demand, and inflexible in monopolistically controlled markets, so that the frequency and amplitude of price changes is, without more, evidence of the degree of monopoly.[137] The difficulty in applying such a premise to the real world is that during the course of a trade cycle some costs change while demand is changing, so that factors other than demand cannot in fact be assumed to remain fixed; furthermore, the elasticity of demand for different products

Mason, *Price Inflexibility* (1938) 20 REV. ECON. STAT. 53; Rothschild, *The Degree of Monopoly* (1942) 9 ECONOMICA (N. S.) 24; *id., A Further Note on the Degree of Monopoly* (1943) 10 ECONOMICA (N. S.) 66.

136. Lerner, *supra* note 135, at 168. It would not do, Professor Lerner points out, "to sacrifice the logic of the science to the irrelevant convenience of the shop keeper."

137. See Means and Galbraith, *loc. cit. supra* note 135, and for a summary of the criticism of their position, NEAL, *op. cit. supra* note 135, ch. 2.

varies greatly through time, and the structure of such demands varies with changes in the level of national income.

Factors of market or of industry organization are thus not the only forces influencing price movements, especially in their response to shifts in demand. To avoid misleading or even nonsensical inferences from statistical correlations, certain limitations should be strongly emphasized in interpreting the trend of oil prices. In the first place, the institutional organization of the petroleum industry, and of the markets for most petroleum products, was radically changed during the thirties. Both public and private control techniques were perfected for most sectors of the industry. Secondly, there were secular increases in the demand for petroleum products, and steady, cost-reducing improvements in the methods of extracting, refining and transporting petroleum products. Finally, there were significant changes in the rate of discovery and of exploitation of new reserves and of new pools.

The most suggestive study of price behavior from the point of view of price flexibility in a series of petroleum markets is the second volume of Professor Joe E. Bain's *The Economics of the Pacific Coast Petroleum Industry*, entitled *Price Behavior and Competition* (1945). He finds a pattern of prices for the Pacific Coast petroleum industry which conforms to the results which would have been predicted analytically on the basis of its structural organization. Every important change in the legal environment, including the relaxation of the Ethyl Corporation's licensing practices after its Sherman Act experience, is reflected in price and market behavior. "Looking at the market structure as a whole," Professor Bain concludes, "it is apparent that a very large proportion of the observed price results and competitive behavior in the California oil industry after 1930 can be fully rationalized in terms of this [changing legal] structure and of the profit-seeking propensity of private business." [138] Production, prices, and price movements were closely correlated with major changes of legal policy, and

138. 2 BAIN, 356.

other aspects of institutional organization. When, early in the thirties, the system of state allowables and of prorationing developed—and this technique was effectively applied in California before it could be established in the Mid-Continent area —production and prices were sharply responsive, as is evident in Figure 1. The N.R.A. period is reflected in the statistical record by clear and stably held price increases; the end of N.R.A., by falls in price and increases in production. The re-establishment in California of firm private production controls, reinforced by the major company buying program, led to a four-year period of price stability, both for crude and for gasoline prices, which ended in 1940, when a plea of *nolo contendere* was entered by the major companies to an anti-trust indictment addressed to their buying program.[139] After 1940, of course, most of the recorded price movements, after a brief period of price weakness, were under war-time control, and the strong upward pressure of war and post-war financial conditions on all prices. One of the interesting aspects of the high and stable prices which characterized this period was their effect in attracting the entry of new firms, and the expansion of older independent firms who, under the majors' buying program, were assured a profitable outlet for their production. This tendency, indeed, had become so pronounced that Professor Bain concludes that "the majors' chagrin at the anti-trust suit may have contained a liberal admixture of a feeling of relief." [140]

A comparable pattern of price variation is traceable in the other regional markets for petroleum products, except in the Pennsylvania market, with its more competitive structure, and more variable pattern of pricing. Prices in California, however, seem to have been both more stable and consistently higher than prices in other areas, reflecting in large part the more effective curtailment program in California during the early thirties, and the impact of "exports" from California at

139. *Id.*, 270.
140. *Id.*, 276.

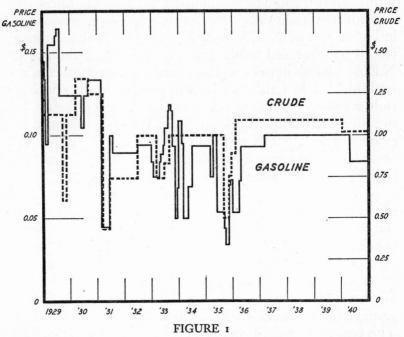

FIGURE 1

The solid line shows the price per barrel of a particular grade of California crude, and the dotted line the Los Angeles tank wagon price for regular grade gasoline.[141]

141. Fig. No. 1 is based on Figure 27, 2 BAIN 56. The crude is Signal Hill 27° gravity. Fig. No. 2 appears in United States Department of the Interior, Minerals Yearbook, Review of 1940 (1941) 967. The Pennsylvania crude is Bradford, the Oklahoma crude is 36–36.9° gravity, the California crude is Long Beach 27–27.9° gravity, and the West Texas crude is 30–30.9° gravity. Fig. No. 3 is adapted from Exhibit 1324 appearing in TNEC HEARINGS, Part 17, facing p. 9951. The East Central Texas crude is 37° gravity and the Texas Gulf Coast is 29° gravity.

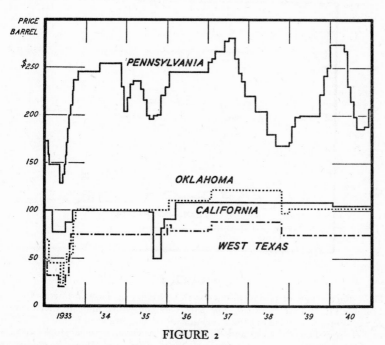

FIGURE 2

Posted Prices of Selected Grades of Crude Petroleum, 1933–1940, by months. Average monthly prices for selected grades of crude. The curve labelled "Oklahoma" represents Oklahoma and Kansas prices.

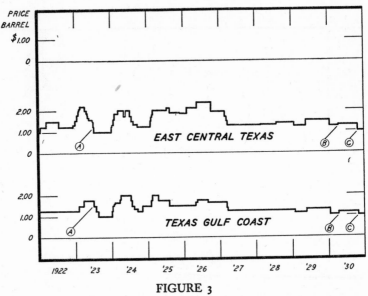

FIGURE 3

Daily fluctuations of posted prices for three grades of Texas crude sold by the Humble Oil and Refining Co. The letters on the figure indicate the timing of certain important events in the development of oil policy, as follows: A. Flood of Oil from Powell-Luling and Big Lake; B. Accumulation of stocks arrested, gasoline market improved; C. Crude in North Texas and Panhandle sold below posted prices; D. Crude sold below posted prices; E. First postings for East Texas, equalizing other prices to East Texas prices; F. Martial law declared in East Texas field—shut in Aug. 17 to Sept. 2; G. Humble reduces its production and prices.

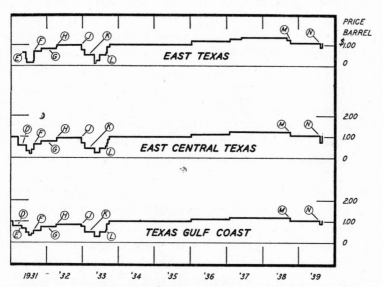

H. Humble meets Mid-Continent's Crude advance and hopes it is warranted and product prices will advance; J. East Texas shut in again—Dec. 17 to Jan. 1; K. East Texas shut in again—April 6 to April 11, East Texas out of control again after reopening; L. President signs Oil Code. Humble looks forward with confidence to the balancing of supply and demand; M. Humble follows Mid-Continent cut. Crude going below posted prices; N. Humble follows Sinclair cut. Texas ordered shut in for 15 days beginning Aug. 15.

lower prices than those which prevailed at home, in the familiar pattern of dumping practices.[142]

However convincing the chronological association of institutional change and price change may be—and it shows up strongly in all three of the above charts—one hesitates to assert that the one caused the other. The connection between particular price patterns and monopoly in the analytical and institutional sense is puzzling to chart statistically, since the course of prices is a function of several variables other than industrial organization. It is difficult, and probably unnecessary, however, to ignore the causal inferences of a study like Bain's; indeed, even Neal, a vigorous opponent of the thesis that concentration causes price inflexibility, concedes that in fact overt business combinations do result in limiting the variation of particular prices, even though such combinations may not show up strongly in gross statistics.[143]

Apart from investigations of movements in oil price series, considered in relation to the special episodes of recent oil history, there have been several elaborate studies of the comparative prices of the major commodities or commodity groups, usually including one or more series for petroleum products. Perhaps the fullest analysis of comparative price flexibility among commodities is that of Nelson and Keim, who find the prices of petroleum products to have been generally among the more flexible prices during the period of their observation, which for most purposes is 1926–1933. Some observations about the period of the thirties are made, and, although these may be read as indicating an altered pattern of price flexibility in petroleum prices for that period, no general conclusions from the Nelson and Keim data are possible about the effect of the changed institutional organization of the petroleum industry on the degree of flexibility of its prices.[144]

142. 2 BAIN, 349.

143. NEAL, *op. cit. supra* note 135, at 134.

144. NELSON and KEIM, PRICE BEHAVIOR AND BUSINESS POLICY, TNEC MONOGRAPH No. 1 (1940) App. I. Similarly, Neal's interesting work (*op. cit. supra* note 135, chs. 5–6), analyzing the relationship between the course of prices and the course of costs, is carried out only for the period 1929–1933.

Professor Mills' recent study plots for 64 commodities the correlation between production and price changes during carefully defined phases of a large number of business cycles, going back in the case of some commodities to 1858.[145] He measures the relative importance of price and of output changes in the response of different industries to industrial fluctuations. So far as the petroleum industry is concerned, his study deals almost entirely with Pennsylvania production, now a minor segment of the national market, and decidedly atypical in its organization and production pattern.[146] While there is some difference in response among the four petroleum series he uses, generally speaking petroleum products appear in his study as showing variability well above the median point for the series in the joint response of price and quantity to cyclical change, the price component of the variation accounting for 98 per cent in the case of Appalachian crude production; 78 per cent, in the case of lubricants (also Appalachian); 66 per cent for a combined petroleum index; and 49 per cent for Appalachian gasoline.[147] About half the sample showed prices fluctuating more than quantities in the course of trade cycles. Since the various petroleum indices used go back to 1914 in one case, 1919 in two cases, and 1891 in the fourth, and are in any event confined to the Appalachian field, Professor Mills' work can contribute little directly to measuring the effect on price policy of the changing economic organization of the petroleum industry. His general conclusion, however, shows wide diversity among products in the variation of their prices and production during trade cycles, and in the relative importance of the price and output components of their variable responses. While output rises almost universally more than price during expansions, and falls less than price during contractions, there is considerable variation among commodity groups, the price factor contributing 16 per cent of the combined fluctuation in value for durable goods, and 96 per

145. F. C. MILLS, PRICE-QUANTITY INTERACTIONS IN BUSINESS CYCLES (1946).
146. *Id.*, 125.
147. *Id.*, 29.

cent for crop products.[148] Mills finds that price flexibility and inelasticity of output are associated, and that where prices are more stable, output fluctuates more. However, this conclusion in its present form supports no causal inferences as to the impact of cyclical forces in the alternative on price or on output for industries of different structural organization, in the absence of information as to varying circumstances of cost and of demand.

Another and perhaps more fruitful approach to the problem of devising quantitative measures of monopoly power is the study of comparative rates of profit. Professor Bain wrote an early article on the subject [149] which proposed to measure the difference between actual monopoly profits and the profits which would prevail under competitive conditions, if "competitively necessary" investment were valued at "competitive" levels. He attempted a rather generalized application of his method in his study of the Pacific Coast industry. His conclusion is that from 1929 onward the over-all profits of the industry, excepting those of non-integrated crude producers,[150] provided "no more than a normal percentage return on actual investment." [151] No inference from this conclusion is permissible, however, even in the absence of any quantitative measure of "normal" returns, since "actual investment" in the petroleum industry contains extensive outlays and inflated entries for reserves, wells, distributing facilities and other capital which would be partially or totally redundant under competitive conditions. Moreover, advertising and other distributive costs are incurred as an alternative to price reductions in a volume which makes the estimate of its "normal competitive profit" a very slippery business. Net returns are affected further by prevailing practices of price discrimination, especially in the export of petroleum products from California at prices below the West Coast domestic price.

148. *Id.*, 48.
149. Cited *supra* note 135.
150. 2 BAIN, 330–332.
151. *Id.*, 347.

Professor Bain makes no attempt to estimate the "competitive value" of the "competitively necessary" investment of the Pacific Coast petroleum industry, in order to provide a base for his comparison of profits. Nor does he attempt more than a subjective guess as to the significance of excess selling costs incurred as a consequence of monopolistic organization of gasoline marketing.[152] In addition, his basic cost data as to crude oil production are those of a Tariff Commission study which, as he points out, counts as costs a good many dubious items, for the purpose of his inquiry, including depreciation, depletion and overheads.[153] The statistical basis of this cost study has been criticized elsewhere.[154] Thus while Professor Bain's study of profit margins is consistent in every way with his institutional analysis of the oil industry on the Pacific Coast, it cannot be said to throw new light on problems of analyzing market behavior, nor to provide simpler and more realistic tools for the measure of monopoly power.

Nonetheless, the ultimate badge of a monopolist should be his ability to react to changes in demand in a more profitable way than a competitive seller. The measure of profit, via the relation of price to the marginal cost of the firm, is the essential principle of Professor Lerner's "test" of monopoly power.[155] And Neal's study reveals a quite distinct correlation between profitability and concentration, during the severe depression period 1929–1933, when changes in the pattern of demand wiped out even the potential profitability of many pure and perfect monopolies.[156]

For the oil industry, the fullest recent account of the rela-

152. *Id.*, 247 ("As a final subjective estimate of the author, it is not inconceivable that distributive costs could be cut at least 1 cent per gallon").

153. *Id.*, 80. See United States Tariff Commission, Report on the Cost of Producing Crude Petroleum (1942) 39, and Supplemental Report (1943). The Tariff Commission's cost estimates are primarily affected by changes in the volume of production. See 1942 Report, 8. There are some interesting but inconclusive cost data in R. B. SHUMAN, THE PETROLEUM INDUSTRY (1940) chs. 3–4.

154. See United States House of Representatives, Select Committee, *loc. cit. infra* note 179.

155. Cited *supra* note 135, 168 *ff.*

156. NEAL, *op. cit. supra* note 135, ch. 6.

tion between prices and costs is presented by the Tariff Commission's cost studies. The result of those studies is summed up in the following table: [157]

TABLE I

Period	Region					All States
	California	Rocky Mountain	Midcontinent-Gulf	Illinois	Eastern	
Average value per barrel at well						
1939	$1.037	$0.853	$0.998	$1.052	$1.440	$1.022
1940	.964	.823	1.002	1.069	1.610	1.018
1941:						
Jan.–Sept.	.988	.893	1.089	1.264	1.858	1.105
1st quarter	.948	.862	1.001	1.144	1.704	1.027
2nd quarter	.991	.901	1.111	1.286	1.858	1.119
3rd quarter	1.025	.982	1.158	1.355	1.992	1.171
Average net cost per barrel at well [1]						
1939	.617	.628	.854	.474	1.300	.785
1940	.619	.554	.838	.473	1.347	.759
1941:						
Jan.–Sept.	.597	.469	.812	.576	1.463	.756
1st quarter	.607	.477	.827	.521	1.431	.754
2nd quarter	.592	.450	.816	.564	1.477	.751
3rd quarter	.587	.470	.828	.627	1.458	.764
Average margin per barrel at well [2]						
1939	.420	.225	.144	.578	.140	.237
1940	.347	.269	.164	.596	.263	.259
1941:						
Jan.–Sept.	.391	.426	.277	.688	.395	.349
1st quarter	.341	.385	.174	.623	.273	.273
2nd quarter	.399	.451	.295	.722	.381	.368
3rd quarter	.438	.512	.330	.728	.534	.407

1. Based on company-interest production, deducting royalties accruing to landowner and other interests.
2. Excess of average value per barrel over average net cost per barrel at well.

The pattern revealed in the table is of considerable interest. A high level of profitability is apparent in California and in Illinois. In California costs are low, due to the richness of re-

157. United States Tariff Commission, Report on the Cost of Producing Crude Petroleum (1942) 2.

sources, whereas price is relatively high both because of the area's geographical isolation from other sources of supply, and because of the more effectively controlled system for determining price and output. Illinois wells, close to their markets, and operating on the low-cost basis of uncontrolled production, are the beneficiaries of a system of basing point price quotation designed primarily to protect the Mid-Continent producers and refiners, and to insulate the Mid-Continent market against dislocation arising from Illinois' uncontrolled production.

This study fills in some of the factual background for Professor Crum's valuable report on the rate of return to equity capital between 1931 and 1936, which indicates that in the petroleum industry as a whole, unlike many others in that period, intermediate-sized companies earned a higher return than very small or very large companies.[157a]

If we are to measure monopoly power, however, we are interested in the relation of price to the marginal costs of each seller, and not in the first instance for fields and industries as a whole. Assuming that each increases his production so long as his additional output earns more than the additional costs associated with it, we need to know the pattern of such additional costs for each firm. A total of costs which includes many items of overhead merely confuses the issue, and cost averages for many wells are worse than useless, for the purpose of revealing monopoly power. Profit as such is not a measure of monopoly; under many circumstances price will exceed average costs for many or all sellers in a competitive market. The crucial evidence of monopoly power from the analytical point of view is a seller's ability to keep price above his marginal costs at the level of output he elects. That power has not so far been measured quantitatively. In view of the inherent difficulties of the task, it is unlikely that it will be measured soon. Meanwhile, we must be content with determinations of monopoly power which rest on a full analysis of market forces in action. Unfortunately, there are as yet no short-cut quantitative substitutes for judgment.

157a. W. L. CRUM, CORPORATE SIZE AND EARNING POWER (1939) 99–101.

PART IV

OIL ABROAD

FOREIGN oil is another whole area of petroleum policy closely connected with the problems arising from the structure and functioning of the industry at home. Foreign oil reserves may be important to American security; at any rate, we think they are, and that is the important thing. Conflict with other countries over access to foreign sources of oil has been and will undoubtedly continue to be a recurring theme of world diplomacy. Imports of foreign oil into the United States are at least potentially significant competition for our domestic industry, and the possibility of such imports, in terms of our tariff structure, helps to set one of the upper limits on the price level which can be established for oil products at home. Exports of American oil, and the purchase of foreign produced oil by American companies, either for their foreign or domestic business, may give rise to agreements and arrangements among American exporting companies, or between American and foreign oil companies, or between the United States and other petroleum producing countries, which can vitally influence the organization of the industry at home. Effective cartelization of the world petroleum industry, with or without governmental supervision, would set up pressures opposing the development of the petroleum industry at home in a more competitive direction. Contrariwise, the weight of the American industry is so great that our abstention could veto plans for dividing world oil markets on a non-competitive basis.

CHAPTER 12

The Foreign Oil Policy of the United States

AMERICAN oil companies have had several types of relationships with other sectors of the world oil industry. Some American companies own oil properties or concessions abroad, either alone, with other American companies, or with foreign companies.[158] Others have contracted with foreign companies for the purchase and exchange of petroleum products, the exchange of information and patent rights, and the division of world markets for particular petroleum products. Some of those arrangements, particularly with German companies, were scrutinized and severely criticized, during the war, as imposing extraordinary restrictions upon the technology of our domestic oil industry.[159] Still other companies are exporters of petroleum products on a massive scale, while some import limited quantities of crude petroleum, especially from the Caribbean. Before the war the United States consistently exported a

158. O'MAHONEY HEARINGS, *American Petroleum Interests in Foreign Countries* (1945); *id., The Independent Petroleum Company* (1946) 377–443; B. T. BROOKS, PEACE, PLENTY AND PETROLEUM (1944); FEIS, PETROLEUM AND AMERICAN FOREIGN POLICY (1944); *id., Order in Oil* (1944) 22 FOREIGN AFFAIRS 616; *id.*, SEEN FROM E. A. (1947) 93–192; *Oil Is the Prize of Victory* (1942) 25 FORTUNE 70; *Socony's World, the Strategy of Oil* (1942–1943) 26 FORTUNE 110, 27 FORTUNE 114.

159. United States Senate, Joint Hearings before a Subcommittee of the Committee on the Judiciary and the Special Committee Investigating Petroleum Resources (S. Res. 36), 79th Cong., 1st Sess., on S. 11, *Foreign Contracts Act* (1945) 47–61; United States Senate, Special Committee Investigating the National Defense Program (S. Res. 71), 77th Cong., 1st Sess., Part 11, 4307 *ff.* (1942); United States Senate, Committee on Patents, Hearings on S. 2303 and S. 2491, 77th Cong., 2d Sess., *Patents* (1942) Parts 1–9, Part 10, index; United States Senate Subcommittee of the Committee on Military Affairs, Hearings under S. Res. 107 (78th Cong.) and S. Res. 146 (79th Cong.), 79th Cong., 1st Sess., *Elimination of German Resources for War* (1945) especially Parts 3, 7 and 10; W. BERGE, CARTELS (1944); BORKIN AND WELSH, GERMANY'S MASTER PLAN (1943) chs. 13, 14; C. EDWARDS, A CARTEL POLICY FOR THE UNITED NATIONS (1945); E. MASON, CONTROLLING WORLD TRADE (1946) ch. 4; M. WATKINS AND STOCKING, CARTELS IN ACTION (1946) chs. 3, 9–11. See Kronstein, *The Dynamics of German Cartels and Patents* (1942) 9 U. OF CHI. L. REV. 643, 10 *id.* 49.

good deal more of all petroleum products than were imported, the figures for 1938 being 194 million barrels of exports against 54 million of imports; for 1939, 189 million barrels of exports against 59 million of imports; for 1940, as the war and our preparedness effort began to show in the pattern of American trade, 130 million barrels of exports and 84 of imports.[160] Our investments in oil properties abroad are substantial, and represent a sizeable participation in the chief petroleum areas of the Middle East, South America and Indonesia.

The oil policy of the government of the United States, while spasmodic, shows a pattern of steady development since the period of a feared shortage after the first World War. Negotiations among the private interests involved, supplemented by occasional diplomatic intervention, succeeded in obtaining for American companies a considerable claim to the oil of South America, the Far East, and in the most controversial of all oil areas, the Middle East. American interests in the Middle East are based on concession contracts of the governments of Iran, Iraq and Saudi Arabia, and on contracts between American and other oil companies.[161] The Standard Oil Company

160. O'MAHONEY HEARINGS, *Petroleum Requirements—Postwar* (1945) 98.

161. In Saudi Arabia and Bahrein, the Arabian American Oil Company and the Bahrein Petroleum Company, until recently jointly owned by Standard Oil Co. of California and the Texas Company, have had exclusive exploration and development rights since 1933. In Iraq, Qatar and Trucial Oman, the Iraq Petroleum Company has had since 1927 a 23¾ per cent American participation, through the Near East Development Co., owned by Standard Oil Company (New Jersey) and the Socony-Vacuum Oil Company; the other shares of the Iraq Petroleum Company are owned by British, Dutch and French interests. In Kuwait, the exclusive concession is held in equal shares by the Anglo-Iranian Oil Company and a subsidiary of the Gulf Oil Corporation, which is bound by its contract with Anglo-Iranian not to market its share of the Kuwait oil in areas in which Anglo-Iranian products are marketed. The first shipment of Kuwait oil on the world market was made in 1946. See FEIS, PETROLEUM AND AMERICAN FOREIGN POLICY (1944) ch. 5; O'MAHONEY HEARINGS, *American Petroleum Interests in Foreign Countries* (1945). In South America and the Far East these five companies, together with the Sinclair Refining Co., the Atlantic Refining Co., and some other major companies, operate in different combinations. See United States Tariff Commission, War Changes in Industry Series, Report No. 17, *Petroleum* (1946) 115–122; O'MAHONEY COMMITTEE, *Final Report* (1947) 32–48; United States Senate, Special Committee Investigating the National Defense Program, under S. Res. 71 (77th Cong., 1st Sess.) 78th Cong., 2d Sess., Report No. 10, Part 15, Section 1, *Petroleum Matters* (1944).

The 1928 "Red Line" agreement, restricting competitive expansion among the

of California and the Texas Company have been until recently the chief American concessionaires in the Middle East, as joint holders of the major contract in Saudi Arabia. In December 1946 their collaboration was widened by the sale of part of their interest to the Standard Oil Company (New Jersey) and the Socony-Vacuum Oil Company.[162] These four American companies acting together are now therefore joint owners of perhaps the largest known field awaiting intensive exploitation in the world. The arrangements which the four companies have made with each other, and with their chief competitor in the Middle East, the Anglo-Iranian Oil Company—a corporation partially owned by the British government—assure the world oil industry an undivided and reinforced phalanx of economic and political power, and constitute a solid preparation for whatever difficulties may arise with local governments or with rival great powers. Furthermore, the extensive cooperation of the four American companies in the Middle East, and their relationship abroad with the Gulf Oil Company, partner of Anglo-Iranian in the Kuwait concession, cannot fail to have long-term repercussions on their relationships in the domestic field.

The government of the United States has recently attempted to articulate a positive foreign oil policy, going beyond the sponsorship and diplomatic protection of private oil interests operating abroad. After a series of skirmishes and alarms, this

participating companies in the Middle Eastern oil contracts, is now in litigation in England, on the issue of whether it is still in effect. New York *Times*, Jan. 12, 1947, Section 3, p. 1, col. 5.

162. New York *Times*, Dec. 27, 1946, p. 25, col. 8; Dec. 28, 1946, p. 22, col. 4; Dec. 29, 1946, Section 3, p. 1, col. 6; Burns, *Second Major Middle East Deal Disclosed* (Jan. 4, 1947) 45 OIL AND GAS JOURNAL (No. 35) 30. This contract carries far-reaching implications. It not only provides for participation in the Arabian concession by two of the strongest Standard companies, but it establishes a continuing supply relationship between American companies and Anglo-Iranian, and sets out by way of private agreement the basis for building essential Middle Eastern pipe lines. Thus the agreement achieves purposes which the United States Government had sought in vain to accomplish during the war [See FEIS, SEEN FROM E. A. (1947) 110–156] but on the basis of unregulated arrangements among strong private companies. Among the many important implications of the agreement is the possibility that the Middle East—an area now entirely controlled by cooperating private companies—will become the base of the world price structure for petroleum products. See Burns, *supra*, at 31.

policy has resulted in the drafting of the main principles of a multilateral international treaty on various aspects of oil diplomacy, and the negotiation in several stages of a preliminary agreement with Great Britain, designed to harmonize the views of the two chief Western oil powers, and to provide the basis for their joint proposals to other countries.[163]

The first version of the Anglo-American oil agreement was signed in August, 1944 as a treaty, and submitted to the Senate by President Roosevelt for ratification. It never emerged from the Senate Foreign Relations Committee, and was later withdrawn for renegotiation in the light of criticisms expressed in the Senate and by the American industry. A revised version was signed in 1945, and has been in the hands of the Senate Foreign Relations Committee ever since. Hearings were held in the late spring of 1947 before the Foreign Relations Committee, but no final action was taken, and at this time Senate approval seems doubtful.

As one of our most thoughtful students of foreign oil policy has remarked, "The reader of the agreement is at first likely to feel as though he were walking among the spaces and angles of an abstract painting." [164] The agreement covers many aspects of oil policy, in a vocabulary so refined by negotiation as to require the drafters' minutes as a handbook of construction. The basic principle of the agreement is that the "orderly" development of the international petroleum trade can best be promoted by international agreement, among all countries interested in the trade, whether as producers or consumers.[165] Therefore, the two signatories agree to propose to all interested oil countries the negotiation of an oil agreement which would establish a permanent international oil body, presumably to be part of the machinery of the United Nations.[166] Meanwhile, the Treaty would establish an interim Anglo-American Com-

163. Feis, *The Anglo-American Oil Agreement* (1946) 55 YALE L. J. 1174; *id.*, SEEN FROM E. A. (1947) 156–190. The text of the first agreement appears in (1944) 11 DEP'T OF STATE BULL. 154, that of the second in (1945) 13 DEP'T OF STATE BULL. 481, and as an appendix to Mr. Feis' article, 55 YALE L. J. at 1188.

164. Feis, *The Anglo-American Oil Agreement* (1946) 55 YALE L. J. 1174, 1182.
165. Anglo-American Petroleum Agreement, Preamble (4).
166. Article III; Article I.

mission to carry out the functions and principles declared in the document.[167]

The Treaty proposes two sets of provisions: the first would establish certain rules of international law to govern the behavior of the signatory governments and their nationals in the international petroleum trade; the second would create arrangements for the joint control of the production and marketing of petroleum products.

In its political provisions, the Treaty is wholly admirable. It would eliminate many of the most irritating international frictions which have arisen out of the competitive conduct of the international oil business. It proposes that adequate supplies of petroleum "should be accessible in international trade to the Nationals of all countries on a competitive and non-discriminatory basis." [168] This provision is a clarification of the "equal access to raw materials" provision of the Atlantic Charter; it applies to all countries, whether enemy or allied in the war; and it gives to the idea of "equal access" its most practicable and satisfactory meaning.

In the second place, it provides broadly that the interests of producing countries should be safeguarded with a view to their economic advancement.[169] This principle is presumably the response of the great oil nations to their unhappy experience in Mexico, and is designed to sweeten the pill of oil imperialism. It is the corollary of the principle, stated in Article II, that "all valid concession contracts and lawfully acquired rights shall be respected, and that there shall be no interference directly or indirectly with such contracts or rights." If the principles of the Treaty are ever proposed to the oil-producing nations of South America and the Middle East, this clause will surely cause heart-searching. Presumably such a treaty provision would come close to conferring jurisdiction on the International Court of Justice over the validity of future confiscations or like sovereign acts. Between Britain and

167. Article IV.
168. Article I (A). This clause represents a revision of the 1944 Agreement, which provided the word "fair" where the word "competitive" now appears.
169. Article I (B).

the United States, of course, it establishes the extraordinary, though altogether desirable, rule that neither government assist in inducing a breach of the contract rights of a national of the other. The agreement to exercise self-restraint in the pursuit of national advantage is carried further in Article II by provisions "that with regard to the acquisition of exploration and development rights the principle of equal opportunity shall be respected; (and) that the exploration for and development of petroleum resources, . . . and the distribution of petroleum shall not be hampered by restrictions inconsistent with the purposes of this agreement."

On the economic side, however, the proposed Treaty adopts the familiar philosophy of cartels. Article IV proposes the immediate establishment of an Anglo-American Oil Commission, operating in close contact with the industry, to consider long-range and immediate problems of mutual interest, and to propose means of achieving their "equitable disposition." The first concern of the two governments in establishing an Interim Commission is to prevent the "deterioration" of "the general petroleum supply situation," a phrase which can only be a euphemism for a fall in price.[170] The duties and responsibilities of the Commission are specified in these terms:

(A) To study the problems of the international petroleum trade caused by dislocations resulting from war;

(B) To study past and current trends in the international petroleum trade;

(C) To study the effects of changing technology upon the international petroleum trade;

(D) To prepare periodic estimates of world demands for petroleum and of the supplies available for meeting the demands, and to report as to means by which such demands and supplies may be correlated so as to further the efficient and orderly conduct of the international petroleum trade;

(E) To make such additional reports as may be appropriate for achieving the purposes of this agreement and for the broader

170. Article IV (1).

general understanding of the problems of the international petroleum trade.[171]

We have had sufficient experience with the functioning of advisory statistical and informational services, and with the administrative "correlation" of supply and demand, to know exactly what the Commission could accomplish, by way of restricting production. In this instance, the proposed Interim Commission might well go beyond the potentialities of the Bureau of Mines, in accomplishing an actual division of markets as between British and American companies.

Large sections of the American petroleum industry are suspicious of the Treaty, and considerable groups, for various reasons, are hostile to it. Independent groups are sensitive to the possibility that the Treaty might result in increasing oil imports into the United States.[172] Others strongly oppose the development of oil production abroad, as a threat to American exports if not to the American domestic trade. The restrictive need for government permission is envisioned as a limit on the freedom of American enterprise abroad. The industry as a whole is vehement in opposing the development of an unduly strong interest in oil on the part of the national government, with its lurking potentiality of "socialism," in the form of government ownership of oil properties or facilities, and of enlarged federal power over the domestic petroleum industry, at the expense of weak state regulation.

Arguments without number gloss but do not define or describe the industry's deep-seated and basically emotional or ideological resistance to the development of a governmental

171. Article IV (3) (A-E). See FEIS, SEEN FROM E. A. (1947) 180–181; E. S. MASON, CONTROLLING WORLD TRADE (1946) 206–208.

172. See Hardey, *A National Policy on Imports and Its Effect on the Domestic Petroleum Industry* (1945) 4 COMPACT COMMISSION BULLETIN (No. 3 and 4) 47; New York Times, Jan. 16, 1946, p. 22, col. 6; (Letter of representative of independent Texas oil producers). The Independent Petroleum Association of America, the Interstate Compact Commission, the Chamber of Commerce and several state bodies, some of which had previously endorsed the Treaty, came out in opposition to it during the last quarter of 1946, inspired by fears of extending government control over the domestic industry. *Storm over the Anglo-U. S. Oil Agreement* (1946) 13 PETROLEUM PRESS SERVICE 224; O'MAHONEY HEARINGS, *The Independent Petroleum Company* (1946) 43–46, 73, 153–176, 336, 400, 412.

oil policy. What the oil men are fighting is an idea—a pattern of relationship between industry and government which violates their notion of the right order of things in a capitalist world. Their stubborn fears are a measure of the difference between American and British or Dutch capitalism, where partnership with the state has always been accepted by business as a convenient device for getting things done.[173]

The Petroleum Industry War Council, a representative body of the industry created to consult with the Petroleum Administrator for War, has formulated a series of statements on the petroleum policy of the United States which seems to express the opinion of the industry.[174] The emphasis of these statements is on the desirability of relying on private companies for foreign oil operations, and of limiting the function of the government to their full diplomatic protection. In view of the importance of British interests in the world petroleum market, special cooperation with the British is recommended, in order to coordinate the policies of the two governments, and to eliminate the possibility—always a source of apprehension in the oil industry—that supposedly "clever" British diplomacy will result in the sudden disappearance of American contract rights in far-off places. On the proposed treaty itself, the Council is significantly silent.

The revised Treaty was drafted after full and laborious consultation with industry representatives. Their particular fears were specifically allayed in the second draft, although the clarifications and revisions seem to make little difference to the meaning of the text. The new text has the specific support of some groups in the industry, although others—and groups of real political influence—are openly opposed. It is hard to see how the agreement could hurt American interests. On the contrary, by stiffening the world price structure, it would undoubtedly make money for American companies. But vague and intangible doubts tenaciously survive. As Geoffrey Crow-

173. FEIS, SEEN FROM E. A. (1947) 164–170; O'MAHONEY HEARINGS, *The Independent Petroleum Company* (1946) 390–394.
174. Conveniently available in O'MAHONEY HEARINGS, *The Independent Petroleum Company* (1946) 427–443.

ther once remarked of an analogous step in the British coal industry, "It is difficult to know which to find more astonishing —the fact that the community has thus encouraged the industry supplying its most vital fuel to hold it up to ransom, or the fact that the industry needed a very great deal of encouragement before it would fully use its legal powers." [175]

175. G. CROWTHER, ECONOMICS FOR DEMOCRATS (1939) 76.

PART V

RESTORING COMPETITION

THE purpose of this paper is to assess the market structure of the oil industry as a whole, using a panoramic view to seek perspective towards the relationship of market forces in action, and their relative importance in the formation of policy as to prices and the level of output. One may summarize its conclusions as follows:

(1) The oil industry is a prime example of an industry in which a monopolistic form of organization is neither technologically nor historically inevitable. Its reorganization in the interest in achieving the social and economic advantages of more competition is entirely within the reach of national policy. Such a reorganization would involve no sacrifice of technical advantage. On the contrary, it should eliminate some of the astronomic wastes of monopolistic competition, and release competitive energies now restricted by monopoly interests.

(2) The essential instrument of economic power in the oil industry is integration, and particularly the ownership by the major companies of transportation facilities; its essential consequence is size. The two forces are correlative and complementary. The great size of the major oil companies is not the result of technological advantage. Smaller units of business organization in the oil industry would not represent a repudiation of "progress," nor an abandonment of the advantages of scale in production. The unit of optimum size technologically bears no relation to the size of the great companies. The companies grew big, as the whole history of the industry testifies, in order to gain the profits of monopoly position. Integration is not a means of achieving economies in production, nor does it result in such economies. It is the basic means of achieving and maintaining monopolistic control over price. Bigness is a

monopolistic force in this as in other markets: it is the end product of integration, as well as an important condition of its successful use.

The key to an effectively competitive reform of the petroleum industry is therefore the separation of the major companies into separate units controlling their four chief functions, production, transportation, refining and distribution, and the further horizontal division of some of the dominant units which would survive a vertical dissolution of the great companies. Freeing the oil industry from the effects of monopolistic size is not a sufficient oil program, but it is an indispensable element of any comprehensive program in the public interest.

CHAPTER 13

Unitization Plus a Program for Freeing the Competitive Potential of the Market

THE starting point in the formulation of an over-all plan for the reorganization of the petroleum industry is the issue of production control. The only form of production control compatible with the public interest would be a federal statute calling for compulsory unitization of the oil fields. Such a statute could fulfill every legitimate criterion of conservation policy, and minimize the risk that conservation would continue to be the mask of restriction and price raising.

To give even a fair promise of success, such a control policy would have to be in the hands of the national government. Production control administered by the producing states can have only one purpose and one end. The risk that even a federal control agency would take on the coloration of the industry with which it is connected is very real. The I.C.C., after all, is more railroad-minded than the railroads, and both the late Bituminous Coal Commission and the various federal oil authorities have had strong industry orientation. Nor could our agricultural policy be described as unfriendly to the interests of agricultural producers. With a federal body, representing the whole country, such attitudes are risks to be guarded against. With state or interstate agencies, representing the oil-producing states, it is a certainty that production controls would be used if possible to limit production and strengthen prices.

The text of a federal unitization statute should have two sets of provisions: one group designed to assure a high standard of operations from the geological point of view, the other, on the side of economic policy, to assure a separation of production from all other phases of the industry, and particularly from transportation.

For unitization is not a remedy for all the ills of the oil industry. Indeed, if unitization were undertaken within the present structure of the industry, it might well heighten rather than diminish the extent of major company control. For the unitized fields would have to be operated on a cooperative basis by a business unit in which all the surface owners were equitably represented, on the basis of their surface acreage, the estimated value of the oil "in place" under their surface tracts, or by some other like formula. Presumably the cooperators would utilize the unit to market oil as well as to produce it, although that by no means follows necessarily. If such units were to be dominated by one or a group of major companies, the competitive potential of the crude oil market would have been appreciably reduced. Unitization as a remedy for waste must therefore be tailored carefully to the economic realities of the oil industry. It is without doubt the ideal procedure of production, geologically. It should be adapted to the structure of the industry in such a way as to stimulate the competitive, and limit the monopolistic pressures in the market. The simplest and most effective way to accomplish this result would be to undertake unitization as part of a general program which included the separation of the major companies into functional units capable of operating in a free market. It might be desirable to fortify the point by extending the principle of the Commodities Clause of the Hepburn Act to all common carriers, including pipe lines and tankers. The Commodities Clause policy—prohibiting the same business from operating in different lines, where such duality of operations might threaten the competitive character of either market—has been found desirable in other fields presenting comparable problems: in commercial and investment banking, in air, ocean, and rail transport, in the relation of air lines to plane manufacturing, and in a variety of other cognate situations.[176]

176. See, among other regulations of this type, United States v. Swift & Co., 286 U. S. 106 (1932); Banking Act of 1933, 48 STAT. 162, 194 (1933), as amended 49 STAT. 703, 709 (1935), 12 U. S. C. § 78 (1940) [see Board of Governors of Federal Reserve System v. Agnew, 67 Sup. Ct. 411 (U. S. 1947)]; Commodities Clause, 34 STAT. 584 (1906), 49 U. S. C. § 1 (8) (1940), United States v. Elgin, Joliet & Eastern Ry. Co., 298 U. S. 492 (1936). See also Interstate Commerce Commission

Another part of a unitization statute would be a series of provisions designed to assure a fair allocation of power and control within the corporations or cooperatives set up to operate the fields on a unitized basis. They might all be made federal corporations from the outset, to assure simple and uniform corporate policy. A provision of technical inspection services, and of administrative procedures for determining the boundaries of oil-producing units would be required, although the administrative controls necessary to carry out a unitization policy would be minimal, and would not extend into the area of commercial practice.

There should be no trouble with a statute along these lines from the constitutional point of view. The notion that "mining is not commerce" has been buried in a long series of cases decided in the last decade. At present it would be more accurate to say that state laws regulating oil production are in a field in which Congress has superior powers. In the silence of Congress, or with the approval of Congress, the states may act, although they may not unduly obstruct, burden nor discriminate against interstate commerce.[177] But when Congress speaks, state laws in the same field are suspended and inoperative.[178] The passage of a federal law controlling the extraction

---

v. Parker, 326 U. S. 60 (1945); Public Utility Holding Co. Act, § 11, 49 STAT. 838 (1935), 15 U. S. C. § 79k (1940); Panama Canal Act, 37 STAT. 566 (1912), 49 U. S. C. § 5 (14) (1940); American Export Lines, Control of American Export Airlines, 4 C. A. B. ECONOMIC REP. 104 (1943); 52 STAT. 1001 (1938), 49 U. S. C. § 489 (1940); Note (1946) 55 YALE L. J. 796; Hale, *Trust Dissolution: "Atomizing" Business Units of Monopolistic Size* (1940) 40 COL. L. REV. 615, 624 ff.

177. The doctrine which begins with Gibbons v. Ogden, 9 Wheat. 1 (U. S., 1824) is in a state of active reconsideration by the Supreme Court. After Parker v. Brown, 317 U. S. 341 (1943), the Court retrieved some lost ground in Southern Pacific Co. v. Arizona, 325 U. S. 761 (1945), asserting its responsibility under the Constitution, in the absence of Congressional action, to protect the national economy against restrictive and burdensome state legislation, by a process of judicial balancing of state and national interests. See Stern, *The Commerce Clause and the National Economy, 1933-1946* (1946) 59 HARV. L. REV. 645, 883; Braden, *Umpire to the Federal System* (1942) 10 U. OF CHI. L. REV. 27.

178. Illinois Natural Gas Co. v. Central Illinois Public Service Co., 314 U. S. 498 (1942); Rice v. Santa Fe Elevator Co. 67 Sup. Ct. 1146 (U. S., 1947); Rice v. Board of Trade, 67 Sup. Ct. 1160 (1947); International Shoe Co. v. Pinkus, 278 U. S. 261 (1929). See Ogden v. Saunders, 12 Wheat. 212 (U. S. 1827). B. GAVIT, THE COMMERCE CLAUSE OF THE UNITED STATES CONSTITUTION (1932) App. D. and

of oil from the ground would eliminate all state laws and regulations deemed within its purview.

If a federal unitization law were passed, no forms of prorationing, or other devices for limiting production to estimates of market demand, would be justified or needed. All conservation interests would be served by the unitization statute. The economic consequences of the rule of capture would be eliminated under a regime of unitization. Beyond that, there is no plausible reason for not allowing market forces to determine the scale of output. Each unified field would be under pressure to produce so long as prevailing or expected prices permitted it to meet its individual costs. Such a rule would assure the community better protection than a method of limiting production to some estimate of what market demand would be at "fair" prices, and it would give the community the further assurance that its oil resources were being used most economically, i.e., that the cheaper fields were being allowed the advantage of their superiority. Production would be greater and more profitable where it was cheapest. It would not be allotted on a per well basis equally among the high- and low-cost units. The norm of production policy would not be an average of costs, nor an intuitive sense of what the fair price should be. The market would fulfill its social function of allocating resources in the most economical way. If a special subsidy were needed in order to preserve the potential output of stripper wells—an unlikely possibility under a regime of unitization—that subsidy could be paid for the stripper wells, without also subsidizing all the other wells of the nation.[179]

E; Biklé, *The Silence of Congress* (1927) 41 HARV. L. REV. 200; Sholley, *The Negative Implications of the Commerce Clause* (1936) 3 U. OF CHI. L. REV. 556.

179. United States House of Representatives, Select Committee to Conduct a Study and Investigation of the National Defense Program in Its Relation to Small Business in the United States, Pursuant to H. Res. 18, Report No. 2015, *Current Problems of Independent Crude Oil Producers*, 78th Cong., 2d Sess. (1944); United States Senate, Subcommittee of the Committee on Banking and Currency, Hearings on S. 502, *To Continue Subsidy Payments*, 79th Cong., 1st Sess. (1945); United States House of Representatives, Special Subcommittee on Petroleum Investigation of the Committee on Interstate and Foreign Commerce, Pursuant to H. Res. 290 (76th Cong.), H. Res. 383 (77th Cong.), H. Res. 58 (78th Cong.), Final Report, *Petroleum Supplies for Military and Civilian Needs*, H. Rep. 2096, 78th Cong., 2d Sess. (1945) 5, 18; O'MAHONEY COMMITTEE, *Final Report* (1947) 8, 57. See R. B. SHUMAN, THE PETROLEUM INDUSTRY (1940) 271 *ff.*

CHAPTER 14

Achieving Free Enterprise under the Sherman Act

It is the conclusion of this study that effective division of the major companies is the key to a successful program for the competitive reorganization of the petroleum industry, and for gaining all the social benefit that might be expected from a policy of unitization. It would be preferable to pursue the remedy through an anti-trust proceeding rather than through legislation and continuing administrative control of the industry. The method of an anti-trust proceeding is surgical. Under judicial control, the companies involved can be reorganized in a single proceeding, and put into a posture where the community could safely rely on the market as its chief agency of economic control. If a competitive organization of the industry is achieved, it could be left free of detailed governmental supervision over its commercial policy. Except for the pipe lines, which would necessarily remain under I.C.C. regulation, it would not only be safe, but preferable, to free the industry of special and continuing administrative direction, apart from the vigilant scrutiny of the Anti-Trust Division of the Department of Justice.

Once effective dissolution is achieved, there is nothing that could be accomplished by administrative control of the market which could not be secured better and more surely without it. By relying for price policy on the competitive forces of a competitively organized market, we should avoid the risks of restrictive and monopolistic policies, and of needless cost, nuisance and waste, which have come so often to characterize our arrangements for the detailed administrative supervision of industry. Moreover, an anti-trust proceeding would permit a desirable discrimination against bigness which would be difficult to achieve under a statute. Effective disintegration of the major companies which constitute monopolistic influences in the petroleum market could be accomplished without prohibiting a small independent refiner from trucking his product to the market, or a small crude oil producer from starting a refinery. The large refining companies would be equally dependent on the market for their supplies of crude—a principle which should deny them an important instrument of monopolistic advantage, if the market itself were competitive in structure.

In attempting to accomplish the full purpose of a disintegration proceeding under the Sherman Act, one should look first to Section 2 rather than Section 1 of the statute. The conception of monopoly in Section 2 has recently been given new promise, which, if fulfilled, should make the Anti-Trust laws a simplified instrument of economic policy, fully adequate to the needs of our time.

The Sherman Act, Chief Justice Hughes once said, "as a charter of freedom . . . has a generality and adaptability comparable to that found to be desirable in constitutional provisions." [180] The great and overriding purpose of the Act is to assure society the advantages which are thought to flow from the competitive organization of industry and commerce. [181] In judging cases under the Act, the Supreme Court is putting less and less emphasis on conduct which hurts individuals by driving them out of business, or restricting their opportunities, and more and more emphasis on arrangements which result in market control, however benevolently exercised.

The idea of monopoly under Section 2 of the statute has the great advantage of neglect. It has been considered separately from Section 1 in very few cases, none of which would stand in the way of a redefinition of the term in the light of our present view of the monopoly problem.

We have learned a good deal about monopoly since the initial dissolution cases in 1911. The word had been given two simple connotations: cases in which there is only one seller of a commodity or services; and cases in which one or a small num-

180. Appalachian Coals, Inc. v. United States, 288 U. S. 344, 359-360 (1933).
181. See, e.g., Associated Press v. United States, 326 U. S. 1 (1945); Fashion Originators' Guild of America v. Federal Trade Commission, 312 U. S. 457 (1941).

ber of persons have the power to exclude competition. But the word "monopolize" in Section 2 of the Sherman Act is not narrowly limited to these two cases. Freedom of entry of new firms into a field is the key to the economists' distinction between competitive and monopolistic markets. Monopolistic markets are those of a single seller, or of a few sellers; and the crucial element of their monopolistic power is a degree of control over the prices they charge. Competitive markets are those of many sellers, no one of whom sells an appreciable fraction of the total supply of the commodity or service on the market, and no one of whom has any discretion as to the price he receives.[182]

Monopoly power is a matter of degree. The extent of the monopolist's control over the prices he charges depends on the availability of substitutes, the nature and elasticity of the demand for his product, the extent to which his product is differentiated in the public mind from that of alternative suppliers, and other factors. Nonetheless, he has a measure of discretion as to the price he charges, while the seller in a perfectly competitive market has no choice but to adapt himself to the market price, as best he may in terms of his internal cost conditions. Both the perfect monopolist, and the seller in markets where there are few rivals, operate in a different economic environment than that of perfect competition. The entry of new firms is at least more difficult and expensive, and therefore the pressure towards a competitive equilibrium is correspondingly reduced. In such circumstances the individual seller naturally does everything he can to increase the degree of his insulation against competitive forces, and thus the extent of his control over his own price policy.

Substantial deterrents upon the entry of new firms is one of the significant hallmarks of monopoly, in economics and now at law. But restrictions on the entry of competitors are evidence of monopoly, not monopoly itself. The new judicial view of monopoly is likely to embrace many market situations

182. WILCOX and others, COMPETITION AND MONOPOLY IN AMERICAN INDUSTRY, TNEC MONOGRAPH No. 21 (1940); NELSON AND KEIM, PRICE BEHAVIOR AND BUSINESS POLICY, TNEC MONOGRAPH No. 1 (1940) Part I, chs. 1–3; and materials cited *supra* notes 3, 30 and 86.

in which effective control of price policy is vested in a small number of large sellers, whether or not those sellers overtly conspire together, and whether or not they act to limit the freedom of others to enter the field. Entry can be deterred, after all, as effectively by the size and entrenched power of existing firms as by the threat of economic warfare.

The Supreme Court is on the threshold of recognizing what the economists call monopolistic competition as the offense of monopoly under Section 2 of the Sherman Act. Monopolistic competition is not uniformly defined by the economists. It is used here to embrace a wide range of market situations in which a small number of large sellers produce the decisive share of market supply. The definition would include the parallel situations where a small number of concerns have determining market influence by reason of their position as buyers. An understanding of the common interest of a few large sellers in parallel action has dispensed with the need of proof of their conspiracy. The economic power inherent in the position a few large sellers dealing in the major part of the supply coming into a market is sufficient to explain many aspects of their behavior—price leadership, fear of spoiling the market, product differentiation, reliance on competitive advertising rather than price competition, and so on. And it shows also that they have powers of price control, and the power to deter or limit the entry of competitors, on which a case under Section 1 and Section 2 of the Act may depend.

Two recent cases, against the background of the last ten years of the Sherman Act in the Supreme Court, mark the new birth of Section 2. The seeds of the doctrine appear in Judge Learned Hand's remarkable opinion in the *Aluminum* case,[183] and in *American Tobacco Company v. United States*,[184] which explicitly approves and supports Judge Hand's opinion, and in some respects carries it into new ground.

In the *Aluminum* case Judge Hand finally interred and re-

183. United States v. Aluminum Company of America, 148 F. (2d) 416 (C.C.A. 2d, 1945). Note (1945) 54 YALE L. J. 860.
184. 66 Sup. Ct. 1125 (U. S. 1946).

versed the old dictum that size is not an offense under the Sherman Act. Size, he concluded, was not only evidence of violation, or a potential offense, as in Justice Cardozo's conciliatory formula of the *Swift* case: it was the essence of the offense. Size, meaning market control, was what competition and monopoly were about. All other aspects of the case were subordinated to the central and decisive fact that the Aluminum Company of America, many years after its patents had expired, made, and then fabricated or sold, over 90 per cent of the virgin aluminum used in the United States. Its arrangements with foreign companies for dividing the world markets were further evidence of monopolizing. That it had engaged in deplorable tactics to prevent other companies from entering the field helped compound the offense. But the case was proved, in Judge Hand's view, by showing the company's market power. It made over 90 per cent of virgin aluminum, and therefore had monopoly power. "The producer of so large a proportion of the supply has complete control within certain limits." [185] The line of the opinion is marred by dicta which somewhat confuse its import. The control of 90 per cent of supply, Judge Hand said, "is enough to constitute a monopoly; it is doubtful whether sixty or sixty-four per cent would be enough; and certainly thirty-three per cent is not." [186]

185. 148 F. (2d) at 425.
186. *Id.* at 424. This formula is having an unfortunate effect, being used literally and out of context. See Comment (1946) 56 YALE L. J. 77, 95, referring to the use in the *Hartford-Empire* decree of the figure of 65 per cent as a benchmark of monopoly. In that instance, if the machines leased by a glass machinery manufacturer produce less than 65 per cent of a particular product, a less severe rule for royalty determination is applied. Moreover, in approving the sale of the government's Geneva, Utah, steel plant to the U. S. Steel Corporation as war surplus, the Department of Justice invoked Judge Hand's analysis of the market power of Alcoa as a "rule," proving that there was no violation of the Anti-Trust laws because the Corporation's steel capacity after acquiring the Geneva plant would be only 32.7 per cent of national capacity and only 39 per cent of Far-Western capacity. New York *Times*, June 18, 1946, p. 1, col. 4.
Judge Hand's analysis of the percentage of the aluminum ingot market controlled by the defendants is perhaps the most important part of the case. Alcoa produced 90 per cent of the virgin aluminum used in the United States. Some it fabricated itself, the rest it sold for fabrication to manufacturers. Imports and the recovery of scrap or "secondary" aluminum constituted the only alternative sources. Both imported and secondary aluminum compete with virgin aluminum,

But the reasoning of the opinion is unmistakable. One of the purposes of the Sherman Act, Judge Hand wrote, "was to perpetuate and preserve, for its own sake and in spite of possible cost, an organization of industry in small units which can effectively compete with each other." [187] The development of the statute has made it entirely clear that certain types of contracts and combinations, creating power over price, are completely outlawed. "It would be absurd to condemn such contracts unconditionally, and not to extend the condemnation to monopolies; for the contracts are only steps toward that entire control which monopoly confers: they are really partial monopolies." [188] The offense of monopolizing under Section 2 of the Act thus includes the acquisition or retention of effective

---

and their availability sets limits upon Alcoa's control of price and output. The court included the aluminum which Alcoa fabricated itself as part of "the" commodity being monopolized, on the ground that all fabrications by Alcoa tended to reduce pro tanto the demand for ingots, and that Alcoa's manufacturing activities directly affected the market for ingots. On the other hand, secondary supplies were disregarded, although they too directly affected the market for ingots, because the volume of secondary aluminum was over a period of years virtually in the control of Alcoa.

"In the case of a monopoly of any commodity [Judge Hand said] which does not disappear in use and which can be salvaged, the supply seeking sale at any moment will be made up of two components: (1) the part which the putative monopolist can immediately produce and sell; and (2) the part which has been, or can be, reclaimed out of what he has produced and sold in the past. By hypothesis he presently controls the first of these components; the second he has controlled in the past, although he no longer does. During the period when he did control the second, if he was aware of his interest, he was guided, not alone by its effect at that time upon the market, but by his knowledge that some part of it was likely to be reclaimed and seek the future market. That consideration will to some extent always affect his production until he decides to abandon the business, or for some other reason ceases to be concerned with the future market. Thus, in the case at bar 'Alcoa' always knew that the future supply of ingot would be made up in part of what it produced at the time, and, if it was as far-sighted as it proclaims itself, that consideration must have had its share in determining how much to produce. How accurately it could forecast the effect of present production upon the future market is another matter. Experience, no doubt, would help; but it makes no difference that it had to guess; it is enough that it had an inducement to make the best guess it could, and that it would regulate that part of the future supply, so far as it should turn out to have guessed right. The competition of 'secondary' must therefore be disregarded, as soon as we consider the position of 'Alcoa' over a period of years; it was as much within 'Alcoa's' control as was the production of the 'virgin' from which it had been derived." *Id.*, 425.

187. *Id.*, 429.
188. *Id.*, 428.

market control. Monopoly power has boundaries; at all times it confronts competition which limits its price—the competition of imported supplies, of alternative commodities, of producers who may be attracted into the market by the high level of prices. Nonetheless the existence of market control will suffice to prove a case under Section 2, unless it can be shown that monopoly power was inevitable, or was "thrust upon" the monopolist. No predatory or illegal tactics need be shown, and no specific evidence of "intent." The court will assume that the monopolist knows what he is doing, and is not sleepwalking. The dicta of the *Steel* case, and of *United States v. International Harvester Company* were disapproved.[189] Judge Hand's opinion is a practical and feasible restatement of the conception of monopoly, giving the law new and far-reaching scope.

This essentially economic approach to the problem of the Sherman Act, which promises drastically to shorten and simplify anti-trust trials, is brought much closer to the situation of the oil industry by the *Tobacco* case. The defendants in the litigation—a criminal proceeding in four counts under both Section 1 and Section 2 of the Sherman Act—were the three great companies which together sell something like three-quarters of all the cigarettes sold in the United States, or about four-fifths of the standard-priced cigarettes, as well as a large volume of other tobacco products. These three companies are not integrated, as are the major oil companies. They buy their raw materials from numerous sellers in tobacco markets scattered throughout the growing areas; then they manufacture their products, and sell to jobbers, and to a lesser extent to dealers, directly. There is no attempt at exclusive selling arrangements, but the major companies have had identical discount allowances for jobbers and dealers at least since 1928. The jury found the defendants guilty of conspiring to restrain trade, of monopolizing, of attempting to monopolize, and of conspiring to monopolize. There was found to be both monopoly and restraint of trade—that is, both Section 2 and Sec-

189. *Id.*, 430.

tion 1 offenses—in the markets for leaf tobacco, where the manufacturing companies bought their raw materials, and in the market for cigarettes. The three big companies used the economic power inherent in their size, the jury found, to buy cheap and to sell dear, and to keep independent competition in the industry to a controlled minimum.

Two of the three big cigarette companies were descendants of the American Tobacco Company ordered dissolved by the Supreme Court as a combination in restraint of trade and a monopoly in 1911. Each of the three big companies made between 20 per cent and 30 per cent of American cigarettes— the percentages varied each year as between the three companies. In 1931, the three companies between them made 90 per cent of the small cigarettes produced in the United States, and in 1939, 68 per cent. The percentage of major company production fell during this period, although their absolute production as a group increased. The major company output did not increase as fast as total supply. There were six small companies, three of which produced only 10-cent brands of cigarettes. These smaller competitors increased their production and their share of the market throughout the depression and post-depression period.

In the country auctions at which leaf tobacco is sold, the major companies in effect chilled the bidding. Their representatives would bid only if all three companies were represented. They were under common instructions as to the top limit of their bidding, and as to the fraction of the supply they needed. Each would bid against the others up to the maximum, to make certain that all three were on an equal footing so far as cost of raw materials was concerned. The companies in effect further eliminated competition in buying by specializing in certain grades of tobacco in which the others would be less interested. The sellers preferred to sell to manufacturers rather than to speculators, since the manufacturers could usually pay somewhat more for the crop. Thus the auctions were in large part ritualistic, for the Big Three had determined in advance the price that would prevail, and the division of the supply between the buyers. They had also established a "substantially impregnable defense," Mr. Justice Burton said, against the entry of competition at their expense.[190]

There was practically no overt evidence of combination or conspiracy in developing this price policy. The jury inferred such an understanding on the part of the big companies out of their continued course of action. Actually, the responses of the major companies to the leaf market did not require agreement to be effective. They represented the kind of parallel action which a minimal concern for self-interest would invariably dictate under the circumstances of the tobacco market. Like the major oil companies buying crude oil, the Big Three had nothing to gain and everything to lose by bidding against each other. Each knew that what he did would influence the conduct of the others. Therefore, by agreement or by dumb show, the representatives of the Big Three bought at auctions in such a way, the Court found, as to dominate the price and divide the supply according to their wishes. It would have been difficult if not impossible for the companies making three-fourths of American cigarettes not to dominate price in a market where they were the chief buyers, and the sellers consisted of thousands of unorganized farmers, who had to sell at whatever the market would bring.

In the cigarette market the court similarly found that the Big Three had the power to control prices and to restrict the entry and development of competing firms. Between 1928 and the date of the proceedings, there had been seven changes in the identical list prices and discounts at which the Big Three sold cigarettes. In each case the change had been announced by Reynolds and immediately followed by the other two companies. Arrangements were made to have all price changes simultaneous in effective date. In 1931, Reynolds raised its list price from $6.40 to $6.85 a thousand. This increase, taking place at the depth of the depression, as the demand for cigarettes and other commodities declined with the fall in national income, was in itself an extraordinary assertion of market

190. 66 Sup. Ct. at 1135.

power. Reynolds said that the purpose of the increase was "to express our own courage for the future and our own confidence in our industry." [191] The President of the American Tobacco Company, however, explained that the increase was made in order to give the companies "the opportunity of making some money." [192] The other two big companies followed Reynolds. If they refused to follow, Reynolds would inevitably have reversed its course, so that they would have gained nothing from refusing to follow. On the other hand, if they followed Reynolds' price lead, they would share the potential profits of the experiment generally with Reynolds, or at worst would lose no more than the price leader. As the spokesman for Liggett and Myers rather naïvely put it, his company thought the price rise was a mistake, but felt that unless it followed suit it would have less money than the others to spend for advertising, and thus be in a position of competitive disadvantage.[193]

The 1931 price rise promptly resulted in a stiffening of retail prices, and a falling off in the volume of all the major sales. The sales of 10-cent cigarettes increased from 0.28 per cent of the total sales to 22.78 per cent in 16 months. At the same time total production fell slightly more than 8 per cent, with the Big Three producing 81.4 per cent rather than 90.7 per cent of the reduced total. Yet the increase in manufacturers' margins was such as to boost profits, despite the falling off in volume, to near-record levels in the worst year of the general depression.

Having discovered empirically that the demand for their product declined in the face of a price increase, the market leaders reversed their course, and embarked on a campaign to regain the market from the 10-cent cigarettes. In January and February 1933 the wholesale price of the leading brands dropped twice, the final figure of $5.50 a thousand being some 14 per cent under the 1931 level of $6.40 a thousand. A market war ensued. The Big Three found that they could hold their

191. *Id.,* 1137.
192. *Ibid.*
193. *Ibid.*

own against the cheaper cigarettes if the price differential were no greater than 3 cents a package at retail, such being the measure of consumers' preferences built up by habit, blend and advertising. When in 1933 the sales of the 10-cent brands had dropped to about 6 per cent of the total, the majors began again to raise their prices, and price increases in 1934, 1937 and 1940 brought the list price back to $6.53 a thousand, slightly above the point at which Reynolds' great experiment began in 1931.

The merchandising methods used in the course of the price war were considered by the Court at considerable length. Big Three salesmen put pressure on dealers to sell the major brands at not more than a 3-cent differential above the 10-cent brands, either by raising the price of the cheaper brands or by lowering the price of the major brands. There was no evidence that the majors attempted to prevent dealers from carrying the cheaper brands, or otherwise to deny them the market. They did not, for example, undercut the price of the 10-cent brands, in order to drive them off the scene. The policy which they sought to enforce was one of a standard price differential of 3 cents, in their own favor.

The jury found the defendants guilty on all counts of the information. The writ of certiorari limited the issue before the Supreme Court to the correctness of the trial judge's charge under Section 2 of the Sherman Act, defining the crime of monopolizing. "Now, the term 'monopolize' as used in Section 2 of the Sherman Act . . ." the trial judge said, "means the joint acquisition or maintenance by the members of a conspiracy formed for that purpose, of the power to control and dominate interstate trade and commerce in a commodity to such an extent that they are able, as a group, to exclude actual or potential competitors from the field, accompanied with the intention and purpose to exercise such power." [194] The writ specified that appellate review was to be confined "to the question whether actual exclusion of competitors is necessary to the crime of monopolization under Section 2 of the Sherman

194. *Id.*, 1127.

Act." [195] The Supreme Court upheld the trial court; the power to exclude actual or potential competition, not the actual exclusion of actual competitors, is a hallmark of the offense prohibited by Section 2.

In this case, resting on both Section 1 and Section 2, the charge of conspiracy and combination was thoroughly mixed up with the charge of monopoly. The trial judge had said to the jury that conspiracy was an essential ingredient of the case, and the Supreme Court put in a precautionary statement to the effect that the case could be regarded as a precedent "only in conjunction with such a combination or conspiracy." [196] But the necessary combination was shown by "unity of purpose," without "formal agreement." A course of dealings, action taken in concert, the result and not the form of combination, were held to be sufficient evidence both of combination and of monopoly. A selective review of what the courts had said on the subject earlier led Mr. Justice Burton to support the view "that the material consideration in determining whether a monopoly exists is not that prices are raised and that competition actually is excluded but that power exists to raise prices or to exclude competition when it is desired to do so." [197] He quoted with approval Judge Noyes' remarks in the Circuit Court opinion in the *Patten* case "that trade and commerce are 'monopolized' within the meaning of the federal statute, when, as a result of efforts to that end, such power is obtained that a few persons acting together can control the prices of a commodity moving in interstate commerce. It is not necessary that the power thus obtained should be exercised. Its existence is sufficient." [198] And he took the occasion expressly to put the im-

195. *Id.,* 1126.
196. *Id.,* 1133.
197. *Id.,* 1139–1140.
198. United States v. Patten, 187 Fed. 664, 672 (S. D. N. Y., 1911). It should be noted that Judge Noyes went on to emphasize that in his view "the power of control amounting to a monopoly must be held by persons acting in concert. No monopoly exists when individuals, each acting for himself, own large quantities of a commodity. Under such conditions none of the evils of monopoly is present." *Ibid.*

In the *Tobacco* case, the Supreme Court referred with approval to United States v. Reading Co., 253 U. S. 26 (1920); Northern Securities Co. v. United

primatur of Supreme Court approval on Judge Learned Hand's opinion in the *Aluminum* case, in which Judge Hand held, in an equity suit, not only that the Aluminum Company had violated Section 2 of the Sherman Act, but that the inducement of self-interest, within the framework of the defendant's market position, was important evidence of its violation.

What emerges from the *Tobacco* case is a new, vital and most promising doctrine—a doctrine which provides the Department of Justice with its best opportunity since the Sherman Act was passed to seek the enforcement of the law on a grand scale, and in ways which might produce not piddling changes in the detail of trade practice, but long strides towards the great social purposes of the statute.

The *Tobacco* case was one, after all, in which the defendants were held guilty on criminal charges—always psychologically more difficult to sustain than civil proceedings—under Section 2 of the Act. There were several defendants, not one as in the *Aluminum* case, yet they constituted a monopoly. The position of Justice Clarke in the *Reading* case, and of Judge Noyes in the *Patten* case have meaning: in law as in economics, and despite the dictionary, monopoly is an affair of several sellers, as well as of one. Parallel action based on acknowledged self-interest within a defined market structure is sufficient evidence of illegal action. Despite the narrow limits imposed on the case by the writ of certiorari, the Court managed to say clearly that the power to control prices *or* to exclude competition is the essence of the offense. In the *Tobacco* case, there were real limits upon the monopolists' capacity to raise the price of cigarettes. The Big Three's price-raising experiment during the depression was far from an unmixed suc-

States, 193 U. S. 197 (1904), and to dicta in United States v. Socony-Vacuum Oil Co., 310 U. S. 150 (1940), as well as to lower court opinions in the *Patten* and the *International Harvester* cases (United States v. International Harvester Co., 214 Fed. 987 (D. Minn., 1914). No direct reference was made at this stage of the opinion to the supposed leading cases on the meaning of Section 2, Standard Oil Co. v. United States, 221 U. S. 1 (1911); United States v. United States Steel Corp. 251 U. S. 417 (1920); United States v. Swift & Co., 286 U. S. 106 (1932); United States v. International Harvester Co., 274 U. S. 693 (1927).

cess, from their point of view, and it took almost a decade before they extricated themselves from the enlarged independent capacity their price policy had created. Their wholesale price passed the 1931 point only in 1940, and for several years the Big Three had to be content with a relatively low—though altogether profitable—price level. In fact, the net result of their policy was to lose, apparently for good, a considerable share of the market, and of their market control, for in 1939 the Big Three sold only 68 per cent of American production, as compared with 90 per cent in 1931.

But the Court refused to be confused. The unintelligent exercise of monopoly power was no proof that it did not exist, within limits set by the market structure and the facts of life. When three companies produce so large a percentage of market supply, that fact alone is almost sufficient evidence that the statute is violated. Ruthless and predatory behavior need not be shown. The actual elimination of small competitors is unnecessary. The big tobacco companies, in the final analysis, pursued a policy which increased the number of their independent competitors, and, on net, strengthened their position. Parallel action, price leadership, a reliance on advertising rather than price competition as a means of inducing changes in each seller's share of the market, and, above all, size—the market position of a small number of large sellers or buyers— these are now key points to be proved in a case of monopoly, or of combination in restraint of trade. From such evidence inferences of combination will be drawn, if cautious pleaders rely on Section 1 as well as on Section 2. But the content of an anti-trust case has been enormously limited and simplified, under Section 1 as well as Section 2. Painstaking search for scraps of evidence with a conspiratorial atmosphere are no longer necessary. There need be no parade of small business men as witnesses, to testify that they have been driven from the trade, and their lives ruined, by the ruthless squeeze of monopolistic pressure. Under the *Tobacco* case, the economic fact of monopoly is very close to being the legal proof of monopoly. The decisive elements are the power to assert a degree of control over price and output in the market as a whole; and the power to deter or discourage potential competition—even, as Judge Hand said, by embracing "each new opportunity as it opened," and facing "every newcomer with new capacity already geared into a great organization, having the advantage of experience, trade connections and the elite of personnel." [199]

More than that is implicit in the case. The power to limit or control the market opportunity of independent sellers is not a major part of the proof required under Section 2. It is, on the contrary, a conclusion derived from the central and fundamental fact of monopolistic power over price. For in the *Tobacco* case it was the Big Three's control over market price which gave them the power to limit, if not to exclude the independent tobacco companies. By raising or lowering their prices together they determined the opportunity available to the independent companies. Such powers inhere in the few large sellers who between them produce the dominant fraction of supply. They are the inevitable economic consequences of size, within the structural framework of a market which attaches particular strategic importance to certain elements of control, and sets limits upon the extent to which prices can safely be raised.

Against the background of these cases, an action against the major oil companies as a monopoly, as well as a combination in restraint of trade, should not face insuperable obstacles. The tobacco market resembles the oil market in certain superficial ways—in the importance of controlling the price at which the major companies purchase their supply of raw material, for example; in the importance of advertising in many forms, and price leadership; and in the major companies' constant solicitude to keep the independents' share of the market within manageable limits. Techniques of control differ. The tobacco industry is not vertically integrated, whereas vertical integration is the key to the monopoly power of the major petroleum companies. Exclusive sales arrangements play no part in the organization of the tobacco industry, nor does control of trans-

199. 148 F. (2d) at 431.

portation facilities. These are differences, of course, which should make the petroleum case easier to establish than that against the tobacco companies.

The issue of numbers is one problem which an oil suit would face. In the *Aluminum* case Judge Hand had remarked in passing that the control of 90 per cent of supply in a market was monopoly, 64 per cent was doubtful, and 33 per cent was almost surely not monopoly. In a sophisticated analysis, the Aluminum Company of America was found itself to produce more than 90 per cent of the aluminum ingot supply. In the *Tobacco* case, three companies together were regarded as a monopoly, under circumstances in which they produced between 68 per cent and 90 per cent of effective supply. The 20 major oil companies together refine and sell at wholesale 80 per cent or more of the gasoline supply, under arrangements of market policy which reflect the same basic interests, forces, drives and habits found objectionable in the *Tobacco* case. The question whether 20 companies is too large a group to come within the definition of monopoly under Section 2 of the Sherman Act would have to be confronted. In Mr. Justice Clarke's opinion in the *Reading* case, long relatively neglected, it was asserted that control by a considerable number of sellers over much smaller fractions of total supply carried with it effective and therefore illegal monopoly power.[200] Actually, all the major oil companies do not operate in any one market. They appear in different combinations, and in much smaller numbers, in different regional markets. In all those markets the policy of price and output which prevails, under the impact of the power of the major companies operating there, is effectively monopolistic in pattern—certainly every bit as monopolistic as the policy declared illegal in the *Tobacco* case. This result, and not a mechanical rule of thumb as to how many sellers can be a monopoly, should be the decisive factor in applying the principle of the *Tobacco* case.

In any event, the remedies of Section 1 should be available

200. United States v. Reading Co., 253 U. S. 26 (1920).

also, in attacking the major oil companies as a "combination," bound together, even without a fixed agreement, by common interests, common action, and parallel responses. The integration of the two sections of the Act achieved by Judge Hand, and approved by Justice Burton, should permit the Act to be applied without great difficulty to the problems presented by the oil industry as a whole.

If the offense under either section is monopoly power in this general sense; and if the most important weapon of monopoly power is size based on vertical integration, then vertical disintegration is the starting point for the process of devising a suitable remedy. It would not be enough to divide each of the major oil companies into four separate corporations, specialized in production, refining, transportation and marketing. There would be an equal case for separating other functions, which present comparable potentialities of market power. Foreign oil investments and the export business require careful scrutiny from this point of view. And so do some of the technologically specialized aspects of the oil business, like the production of synthetic rubber and other chemicals. Similarly, a plan of competitive reorganization for the oil industry would necessarily have to deal with problems of market control through horizontal as well as vertical integration. If the oil fields were unitized, there would be a market of at least a hundred major producers, and many more minor producers of crude petroleum. If such a group of sellers had to deal with the refining units of the present majors as purchasers, supplemented by such independent refiners as now exist or could soon spring into existence, the crude market would be dominated by the buying power of the few great refining corporations. The present concentration of refining capacity, and especially of advanced refining technology, would make vertical division of the major companies an insufficient remedy. The principle to be pursued in drafting a detailed reorganization plan must be to see to it that no segment of the market structure as reestablished after the proceeding would be controllable by a few large units, either as buyers or sellers.

On the side of distribution, the main problem to be encountered, once existing wholesale and retail facilities are released from present tying arrangements, would be the future of brands. The number of sellers would presumably be large, and the number of wholesale and retail distributors effectively larger than it is today. Would the highly advertised national brands decline in importance? Would gasoline be sold in bulk at uniform chemical standards to distributors who would market it under their own names? Certainly an increase in the effective number of independent sellers would tend very quickly to reduce the present importance of branding, and the present value of brand names. The costs now associated with branding are an index of monopoly in Chamberlin's sense, and perhaps in Lerner's as well. Nonetheless the right to use trade names would be one of the property interests to be disposed of in an anti-trust decree. Perhaps the proper remedy would be to suppress existing trade names altogether, on the ground (familiar in patent cases) that they have been used as instruments of monopoly power.

Devising a suitable dissolution decree in the light of these principles presents no insuperable technical obstacles. The courts can employ expert assistants as Special Masters in drafting the decree, and as Receivers in carrying it out. Voting trusts and like devices can be used to insure a separation of control pending the reorganization of financial structures and the permanent redistribution of ownership and debt interests. The courts have an ample experience in corporate recapitalizations and reorganizations, both in insolvency proceedings, and in proceedings to enforce the anti-trust laws and statutes like the Public Utility Holding Company Act, the Interstate Commerce Act, and other regulatory statutes.

Thus the doctrine and the procedural devices are at hand which could justify a program of competitive reorganization in the oil industry. Nonetheless, such a program is strongly resisted. Although the dissolution of monopolistic organizations is a familiar remedy in anti-trust history, each new application of it comes with a shock, and meets the natural unwillingness of judges to do anything drastic except to words.[201]

The commonly cited objection to the policy of dividing big corporations into their component units of technological effectiveness—and it is an objection widely shared—is that it would be a step "backward," that it is technologically regressive, and represents only a wistful and sentimental yearning for an era of small business, gone beyond recall. When the spokesmen of such views become specific, they often say that such functional separations would increase costs, by eliminating the supposed economies of integration and adding to the consumer's price the profit charged at each separate stage of production.[202]

One part of this contention is quite simple to deal with. It seems to rest on an obvious mistake as to the power of a competitive seller over the prices he charges for his goods or services. The chief purpose of a plan of dissolution in the oil industry would be to accomplish a structural change in the organization of markets, so that each individual company would have a good deal less power than before over the prices at which it buys crude oil and sells gasoline and other products. It could be expected that no seller would control a sufficiently large part of the supply as to be able even within a range to fix the price at which he sells. The reorganization of the oil industry called for by such a plan would require no new services, and no substantial new capital outlays. On the contrary it should eliminate the need for many of the wasteful and unproductive expenditures which now characterize the industry. It should permit much capital now used restrictively to be used competitively. The flow of funds into the industry should un-

---

201. Black, *Oil Pipe Line Divorcement by Litigation and Legislation* (1940) 25 CORN. L. Q. 510; Hale, *Trust Dissolution: "Atomizing" Business Units of Monopolistic Size* (1940) 40 COL. L. REV. 615. See WILCOX, COMPETITION AND MONOPOLY IN AMERICAN INDUSTRY, TNEC MONOGRAPH No. 21 (1940) 309 ff.; Comment (1946) 56 YALE L. J. 77. Also A. R. Oxenfeldt, *Monopoly Dissolution: A Proposal Outlined* (1946) 36 AM. ECON. REV. 384.

202. United States House of Representatives, Hearings before Subcommittee No. 3 of the Committee on the Judiciary, 76th Cong., 1st Sess., on H. R. 2318, *Oil Marketing Divorcement* (1939) 211, 215-216, 219, 231, 287, 302.

der such circumstances be more sensitive to the pull of alternative possible uses, and to factors of comparative productivity and efficiency. At the present time, the petroleum industry earns an adequate, not to say handsome return on its total capitalization, including all the waste and duplicated capital incident to its monopolistic organization. It is hard to see why market forces governing price should yield a *higher* return on the capital invested in the oil industry, after the industry's power to change monopoly prices had been substantially *reduced*. The rate of return on the capital invested in the industry would hardly increase because the capital was divided among smaller corporate units, each with less power over the prices it charged.

The second phase of the so-called economic objection to disintegration is that disintegration would increase costs by denying the industry economies of the large scale:—better utilization of managerial skills, the advantages of the research facilities of large corporations, and whatever other economies or diseconomies are supposed to flow from common control, forward planning in industrial operations, and so on.[203]

So far as research is concerned, there is already a considerable separation and specialization of research functions in the oil industry. There are important independent engineering firms in the industry, operating on fees. There is no reason why the trend to put industrial research on an economic basis should not grow. Research and engineering firms selling their ideas competitively in a larger market should be at least as productive, and perhaps more productive, than the present research departments of large companies, a considerable part of whose efforts are given over to creating apparent differences in gasoline, necessarily a standardized commodity, without interfering with its standardization. In any event, the costs of separate research programs in the several phases of the industry—exploration, extraction, refining, storage and transportation—would not in any sense be beyond the reach of the sub-

203. *Id.*, 241-242, 287-288.

stantial companies which would emerge from a dissolution proceeding in the oil industry.

As for the economies and efficiencies of the large scale of production, that basic article of the American credo, it seems plain on closer inspection that in the oil industry as in many other cases of vertical integration, they consist more of the profits of monopolistic position and price policy than of actual economies in the sense of cost advantages.[204] Independent units at each stage of the industry claim a unit cost advantage based on their relative smallness. Certainly the effective pressure of independent companies in every phase of the industry, and the elaborateness of the major companies' efforts to contain and offset them, seems to belie the contention that there are substantial economies of integration in the sense of cost advantages. There is no apparent reason, for example, why a refinery should distill gasoline at a lower unit cost, because it is owned by a corporation which also owns tankers, filling stations and pipe lines. Such has not been the general experience with vertical integration, apart from the problem of monopoly. The steel plants of the International Harvester Company and the Ford Motor Company do not exist because they can make steel more cheaply than it can be bought, but as a threat with which to assure those two companies, and others in like position, of a favorable position as buyers in the monopolistic market for steel.[205]

There is a third claim of economy for integration: that it permits cheaper access to the money markets. The argument is that bigger companies can raise funds more cheaply than smaller ones. What this contention comes down to is that imperfections in the organization of our capital markets justify or require imperfections in the organization of industry. The argument is not very plausible for the oil industry, which has never suffered from a shortage of capital. On the contrary, it

204. See A. R. BURNS, THE DECLINE OF COMPETITION (1936) ch. 9, *passim.*
205. BLAIR AND REESIDE, PRICE DISCRIMINATION IN STEEL, TNEC MONOGRAPH No. 41 (1941) 25 *ff.*; Blair, *Price Discrimination in Steel* (1943) 33 AM. EC. REV. 369.

has been an expanding and attractive industry for both speculative and long-term investment.

Finally, it is objected that disintegration would disturb or destroy the market value of outstanding securities, and shake the faith of investors in all industry. This objection means in effect that it would be immoral of government to enforce the Sherman Act by denying monopoly the profits of monopoly, and the capitalization thereof. It is an extraordinary objection, which if accepted would make the Sherman Act totally nugatory. In any event, it is not an objection of overwhelming practical moment, in the face of the financial markets' reaction to the reorganization of the utility holding companies, against which the same pleas were made. The securities of utility holding companies, and of utility operating companies, forced by the Public Utility Holding Company Act to undertake strenuous reorganization, are more than holding their own in the securities markets. The fears of disastrous collapses in values simply did not materialize. The glass machinery and container industries, recently under drastic anti-trust attack, have had the same financial experience.[206]

206. See Blair-Smith and Helfenstein, *A Death Sentence or a New Lease on Life?* (1946) 94 U. OF PA. L. REV. 148, and Comment (1946) 56 YALE L. J. 77, 97; and, contrariwise, e.g., United States House of Representatives, *supra* note 202, at 239, 286–287 (in opposition to divorcement legislation).

CHAPTER 15

Other Aspects of a Competitive Program

THE first two planks of a competitive program for the oil industry, then, are compulsory unitization, and both vertical and some horizontal division of the major companies into at least their four separate functions of production, refining, transportation and distribution. A divorcement of marketing alone, often considered as a remedy, would be inadequate, since it would permit the major companies to dominate the retail market as sellers. Under such circumstances, they would have as much control as they now have of the supply coming forward for retail sale.

Other aspects of public control policy in relation to the oil industry would require consideration even if unitization and disintegration were undertaken. The re-activation of Section 3 and Section 7 of the Clayton Act, dealing with tying arrangements and with the process of corporate combination, could make a useful long-term contribution to the cause of competition in petroleum. Perhaps the process of judicial nullification has gone so far in the case of Section 7 as to require legislative action.[207] In that event, the amendments proposed by the Federal Trade Commission, and supported in the Final Report of the Temporary National Economic Committee, should be adequate for the purpose.[208]

A policy of competition at home carries certain corollaries for our international oil policy. When the literature about in-

207. Arrow-Hart & Hegeman Electric Co. v. Federal Trade Commission, 291 U. S. 587 (1934); United States v. Republic Steel Corp., 11 F. Supp. 117 (N. D. Ohio, 1935).

208. Federal Trade Commission, Final Report on the Chain-Store Investigation, 74th Cong., 1st Sess., S. Doc. No. 4 (1934); *id.,* Growth and Development of Chain Stores, 72d Cong., 1st Sess., S. Doc. No. 100 (1932); Unites States House of Representatives, Hearings before Subcommittee No. 3 of the Committee on the Judiciary, on H. R. 2357, 79th Cong., 1st Sess., *To Amend Sections 7 and 11 of the Clayton Act,* Serial No. 8 (1945); *id.,* Committee on the Judiciary, 79th Cong., 2d Sess., Report No. 1820, to accompany H. R. 5535, *Amending Sections 7 and 11 of the Clayton Act* (1946).

ternational oil policy is parsed into its ultimate components, it seems to boil down to these two propositions:

(1) For security reasons, as well as economic reasons, we should have "equal access" to foreign produced oil. Equal access means both the right to buy at non-discriminatory prices, and the privilege for our industry to compete on equal terms with the oil industry of other nations for concessions and production rights in undeveloped areas of the world. In this category, there are the remarkable and altogether desirable provisions of the pending Anglo-American Oil Treaty, in which both signatories solemnly agree in effect not to steal the oil concessions of each other's nationals.

(2) In order to introduce "order" into the world oil industry, statistical and research bodies are to be established, "recommending" a suitable level of oil output in different producing areas, in terms of market demand, and also "recommending" appropriate sources of supply for different markets. Behind the rhetoric and persiflage of this argument (represented in Article IV of the pending Treaty), there stands a familiar policy of restricting competition, maintaining or enhancing prices, and controlling output. Such a policy would be an extension of our present domestic system of controlling output, with refinements of technique which would make the controls more efficient.

While we have a considerable stake in the first part of such an oil policy, we have an even stronger stake in repudiating the second part. Our non-participation in international market control schemes should go a long way towards making them unenforceable, if our diplomacy succeeds in its present ambitious plans for keeping world markets open, and enlarging the area of multilateral trade.

Equally, we should prevent the Webb-Pomerene Act from being used at all by domestic corporations in combination with foreign companies, and from being used restrictively by American companies acting together abroad.[209] Oil industry

209. See O'Mahoney Hearings, *Final Report* (1947) 44 *ff*. Gilbert, and others, Export Prices and Export Cartels, TNEC Monograph No. 6 (1940); Diamond,

experience with that statute adds to the general case for repealing it. Moreover, the relations between domestic and foreign oil companies in the past have been such as to reinforce Senator O'Mahoney's proposals for a Foreign Contracts Registration Act, and perhaps more severe limitations on international arrangements in restraint of trade.[210]

The operation of American companies abroad presents specialized issues for consideration and decision. Manifestly, it would not serve a useful purpose to require a separation of refining and production, for example, under the circumstances of the industry in Saudi Arabia. Yet the interconnections between the foreign and domestic operations of the same company may raise problems, in the light of the general purposes of our law governing industrial organization. The dominant consideration in approaching the issue should be the effect of foreign oil operations on the freedom of the foreign and domestic commerce of the United States. A flat rule prohibiting the same company from operating both at home and abroad may be ultimately desirable, but the case for such a rule seems weaker than the case against other forms of integration.

Finally, both our foreign and our domestic oil policies would be powerfully served by the transfer of petroleum products to the free list, and the elimination of all quotas or other quantitative limits on imports.[211] Our oil industry is

The Webb-Pomerene Act and Export Trade Associations (1944) 44 Col. L. Rev. 805; MacBride, *Export and Import Associations as Instruments of National Policy* (1942) 57 Pol. Sci. Q. 189; Oseas, *Antitrust Prosecutions of International Business* (1944) 30 Corn. L. Q. 42; Schilz, *Post-War Operations of Export Associations under the Webb and Sherman Laws* (1943) 31 Va. L. Rev. 613; Note (1940) 49 Yale L. J. 1312. See United States Alkali Export Ass'n v. United States, 325 U. S. 196 (1945); De Beers Consolidated Mines v. United States, 325 U. S. 212 (1945); United States Senate, Special Committee to Study Problems of American Small Business, under S. Res. 28, 79th Cong., 2d Sess., Report of Foreign Trade Subcommittee, *Small Business and Webb-Pomerene Act*, Senate Subcommittee Print No. 11 (1946).

210. S. 11, 79th Cong., 1st Sess. A bill to protect the foreign relations and to promote the trade and commerce of the United States. See United States Senate, Joint Hearings before a Subcommittee of the Committee on the Judiciary and the Special Committee Investigating Petroleum Resources, 79th Cong., 1st Sess., *Foreign Contracts Act* (1945).

211. Before 1932 both crude petroleum and its refined products were on the free list, and imports, mainly of Mexican crude oil, were important. The Revenue Act of 1932 imposed import taxes on crude petroleum and, at a higher rate,

hardly an infant industry, requiring subsidy during its swaddling period. So long as there are even possible shortages of oil at home, it is desirable in peace time to use as much foreign oil as is feasible. And the pressure of foreign oil on the domestic price structure would add to the quantum of competition in the oil markets. It is time, and long since, to dismiss the ancient red herring of comparative wage scales from tariff controversies. If our crude oil is expensive in terms of world prices, it is not because of our wage scales, but because of the staggering inefficiency in extractive methods which we continue to tolerate in the name of the rule of capture and the system of prorationing; and because of the impact of monopolistic organization on the oil industry's structure of costs and prices. The remedy for such wastes is not more and more protection, but improvements in efficiency, adopted under the goad of competition.

on its liquid products. The Trade Agreement of 1939 with Venezuela under the Trade Agreements Act of 1934, as extended [48 STAT. 943 (1934), 50 STAT. 24 (1937), 54 STAT. 107 (1940), 19 U. S. C. §§ 1351–1354] reduced the excise tax on crude petroleum by 50 per cent to 10½ cents per barrel, for a quota equal in each year to 5 per cent of the quantity processed in domestic refineries during the preceding year [54 STAT. 2375, 2387, 2451, 2456]; United States Tariff Commission, War Changes in Industry Series No. 17, *Petroleum* (1946) 9–10; O'MAHONEY HEARINGS, *The Independent Petroleum Company* (1946) 153–176.

APPENDIX

THE principal parts of Sections 1 and 2 of the Sherman Act [26 Stat. 209 (1890), 15 U.S.C. §§1–2 (1940)] are as follows:

An act to protect trade and commerce against unlawful restraints and monopolies.

Section 1. Every contract, combination in the form of trust or otherwise, or conspiracy, in restraint of trade or commerce among the several States, or with foreign nations, is hereby declared to be illegal. Every person who shall make any such contract or engage in any such combination or conspiracy, shall be deemed guilty of a misdemeanor, and, on conviction thereof, shall be punished by fine not exceeding five thousand dollars, or by imprisonment not exceeding one year, or by both said punishments, in the discretion of the Court.

Section 2. Every person who shall monopolize, or attempt to monopolize, or combine or conspire with any other person or persons, to monopolize any part of the trade or commerce among the several States, or with foreign nations, shall be deemed guilty of a misdemeanor, and, on conviction thereof, shall be punished by fine not exceeding five thousand dollars, or by imprisonment not exceeding one year, or by both said punishments, in the discretion of the court.

TABLE OF CASES

References are to pages and footnotes

TABLE OF PROPER NAMES

References are to pages and footnotes

INDEX

References are to pages and footnotes